Coding for Digital Recording

By the same author

The art of digital audio
The art of digital video

Coding for Digital Recording

John Watkinson

Focal Press
London & Boston

Focal Press
is an imprint of Butterworth Scientific

 PART OF REED INTERNATIONAL P.L.C.

First published 1990

British Library Cataloguing in Publication Data

Watkinson, John
  Coding for digital recording.
  1. Sound Recording and reproducing. Digital techniques
  I. Title
  621.3893

ISBN 0-240-51293-6

Library of Congress Cataloging in Publication Data

Watkinson, John.
  Coding for digital recording/John Watkinson.
      p.   cm.
  ISBN 0-240-51293-6:
  1. Sound—Recording and reproducing—Digital techniques.
I. Title.
TK7881.4.W383   1990
621.389'3—dc20   89-71497
                                                      CIP

Cover and text illustrations drawn by TecSet Ltd., Wallington
Photoset by Genesis Typesetting, Borough Green, Kent
Printed in Great Britain at the University Press, Cambridge

Preface

Mankind has progressed through various eras, each marked by the development of some skill which had such far reaching effects that society was irrevocably changed.

From the first stone age tools, through the working of metal, through the discovery of the principles of navigation and the great age of exploration that followed, there has always been some vital element that made it possible.

Perhaps some future historian will classify this as the digital age, when everyday processes increasingly came to be performed using discrete numbers. Television pictures, financial transactions, weather forecasting, Compact Disc – the list seems endless, but all have in common with digital computers the need for that vital element, which is the ability to reliably and economically record great volumes of discrete numbers.

The principles of numerical coding can be found in this book, beginning with magnetic and optical physics, progressing through channel coding and error correction to end with some practical examples of current technology.

This is not a conventional book, as it combines physics, pure mathematics and engineering without demanding a background in any of those disciplines. I imagine few books would address topics ranging from audio to computers via video and instrumentation, and yet still be relevant to bar codes in the supermarket and the magnetic stripe on your credit card. There is no place for jargon in such a wide field and thus each concept will be explained in plain English with the necessary terminology defined. Mathematical expressions are used as a last resort. There are few stated facts since these are generally meaningless in isolation. Instead there are explanations, arguments and mechanisms from which most relevant facts can be deduced now or in the future.

Conventional or not, the goal of this book is to help the reader gain an insight into the way abstract mathematics solves engineering problems. This unholy alliance of the pure and the practical is for me one of the most fascinating aspects of the subject.

John Watkinson
Burghfield Common, England
January 1990

Contents

Chapter 1   Why digital recording?   1

1.1   The advantages of digital recording   1
1.2   A short history   5
1.3   Some typical machines outlined   6
1.4   Disadvantages   8

Chapter 2   Digital magnetic and optical recording   9

2.1   Magnetic recording   9
2.2   Head noise and head-to-tape speed   10
2.3   Basic digital magnetic recording   12
2.4   Fixed heads   13
2.5   Flying heads in disk drives   15
2.6   Playback   17
2.7   Azimuth recording and rotary heads   22
2.8   Equalization   24
2.9   Types of optical disk   25
2.10 Optical theory   27
2.11 The laser   31
2.12 Polarization   32
2.13 Thermomagneto-optics   34
2.14 Optical readout   36
2.15 Structure of laser drive   39

Chapter 3   Channel coding   41

3.1 Shortcomings of recording channels   41
3.2 Jitter windows   43
3.3 Simple codes   47
3.4 Group codes   59
3.5 Tracking signals   61
3.6 Convolutional RLL codes   61
3.7 Randomized NRZ   64
3.8 Partial response   65
3.9 Graceful degradation   70
3.10 Synchronizing   72

Chapter 4   Error correction   79

4.1 Sensitivity of message to error   79
4.2 Error mechanisms   80
4.3 Error handling   81
4.4 Interpolation   82
4.5 Noise and probability   83
4.6 Parity   86
4.7 Wyner–Ash code   89
4.8 Crossword code   91
4.9 Hamming code   91
4.10 Hamming distance   95
4.11 Applications of Hamming code   99
4.12 Cyclic codes   101
4.13 Burst correction   110
4.14 Fire code   112
4.15 B-adjacent code   119
4.16 Reed–Solomon codes   121
4.17 Interleaving   130
4.18 Crossinterleaving   135
4.19 Editing interleaved recordings   137

Chapter 5   Applications   141

5.1 PCM adaptors   141
5.2 Open reel digital audio recording   146
5.3 ¼ inch ProDigi format   152
5.4 Introduction to RDAT   158
5.5 Recording in RDAT   167

5.6   DDS–RDAT as a data storage medium   173
5.7   The Compact Disc   179
5.8   CD frame contents   185
5.9   CD player structure   191
5.10 CDROM   196
5.11 Digital video recorders   200
5.12 Audio in D-1 and D-2   208
5.13 Error correction in D-1 and D-2   209
5.14 Concealment and shuffle   212
5.15 Defect handling in disks   213
5.16 Bad block files   214
5.17 Sector skipping   215
5.18 Defect skipping   215
5.19 Revectoring   217
5.20 Error correction in disks   218
5.21 Defect handling in WORM disks   219

Index   221

Inside the back cover of this book is a seven-bit cylindrical Venn diagram, which is further discussed on page 98.

1

Why digital recording?

1.1 The advantages of digital recording

In its purest form, recording simply delays information, often so that it can be processed at some convenient later time. Information takes many forms but always falls into one of two categories: discrete or continuous. Pure logic is only concerned with the truth or falsehood of some statement, and thus the information is binary. Most alphabets have a finite range of symbols and can be completely conveyed by a limited range of integers, as is done in ASCII. Most other types of information are continuous, both in the parameter measured and in the way it changes with respect to time; this kind of information is usually referred to as analog.

There is a fundamental difference between the way these two kinds of information behave in the presence of degradations due to real recording or transmission processes. In an analog system information is conveyed by the infinite variation of some continuous parameter such as the voltage on a wire or the strength of flux. When it comes to recording, distance along the medium is a further analog of time. However much the signal is magnified, more and more detail will be revealed until a point is reached where the actual value is uncertain because of noise. A parameter can only be a true analog of the original if the conversion process is linear, otherwise harmonic distortion is introduced. If the speed of the medium is not constant there will not be a true analog of time.

It is a characteristic of an analog system that the degradations at the output are the sum of all the degradations introduced in each stage through which the signal has passed. This sets a limit to the number of stages a signal can pass through before it becomes too impaired to be of use. Down at signal level all impairments can be reduced to the addition of some unwanted signal, such as noise or distortion, and timing instability such as group-delay effects and jitter. In an analog system such effects can never be separated from the original signal; in the digital domain they can be eliminated.

In a digital recording system the information is in binary form. The signals sent have only two states, and change at predetermined times according to a stable clock. If the binary signal is degraded by noise, this will be rejected at the receiver since the signal is judged solely on whether it is above or below some threshold. However, the signal will be conveyed with finite bandwidth and this will restrict the rate at which the voltage changes. Superimposed noise can move the point at which the receiver judges that there has been a change of state. Time instability also has this effect. This instability is also rejected because, on receipt, the signal is reclocked by the stable clock and all changes in the system will take place at the edges of that clock. Figure 1.1 shows that however many stages a binary signal passes through, it still comes out the same, only later. It is possible to convey an analog waveform down such a signal path.

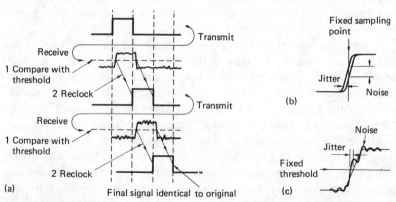

Figure 1.1 (a) A binary signal is compared with a threshold and reclocked on receipt, thus the meaning will be unchanged. (b) Jitter on a signal can appear as noise with respect to fixed timing. (c) Noise on a signal can appear as jitter when compared with a fixed threshold

That analog waveform has to be broken into evenly spaced time elements (a process known as sampling) and then each sample is expressed as a whole number, or integer, which can be carried by binary digits (bits for short). Figure 1.2 shows that the signal path may either convey sample values in parallel on several wires, where each wire carries a binary signal representing a different power of two, or serially in one channel at higher speed, a process called pulse code modulation (PCM).

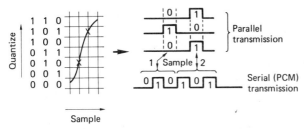

Figure 1.2 When a signal is carried in numerical form, either parallel or serial, the mechanisms of Figure 1.1 ensure that the only degradation is in the conversion processes

In simple terms, an analog signal waveform is conveyed in a digital recorder as if someone had measured the voltage at regular intervals with a digital voltmeter and written the readings in binary on a roll of paper. The rate at which these measurements are made and the accuracy of the meter now wholly determine the quality of the system because once a parameter is expressed as discrete numbers those numbers can be conveyed unchanged through a recording process. This dependence on the quality of conversion is the price paid to make quality independent of the signal path.

A magnetic head cannot know the meaning of signals which are passed through it so there is no distinction at the head/medium interface between analog and digital recording. Thus a digital signal will suffer all the degradations that beset an analog signal: particulate noise, distortion, dropout, modulation noise, print-through, crosstalk, and so on. However, there is a difference in the effect of these degradations on the meaning of the signals. As stated, digital recording uses a binary code and the presence or absence of a flux change is the only item of interest. Provided that flux change can generate a playback pulse which is sensibly bigger than the noise, the numerical meaning will be unchanged by reasonable distortions of the waveform. In other words, a bit is still a bit whatever its shape. This implies that the bits on the medium can be very small indeed and can be packed very close together to achieve economy of operation.

Large disturbances of the recording, such as dropout or severe interference, may cause flux changes to be missed or may simulate ones which did not exist. The result is that some of the numbers recorded will be incorrect. In numerical systems provision of an error-correction system is feasible; in analog systems it is not. If an error correction system is necessary it may be made to work harder by increasing the packing density which results in a greater raw error rate. The increase in density more than compensates for the need to store redundancy. It is probably true to say that, without error-correction systems, high density digital recording would not be technically feasible.

In the digital domain, signals can be easily conveyed and stored in circuitry. Speed variations in recorders cause the numbers to appear at a fluctuating rate. The use of a temporary store allows those numbers to be read out at constant rate, a process known as timebase correction.

The main advantages of digital recording can be summarized as follows (they are not in order of importance because this will change with the application):

★ The quality of a digital recording is independent of the head and medium in a properly engineered system. Frequency response, linearity and noise are determined only by the quality of the conversion processes. Exceptional dynamic range and linearity are readily achieved, combined with freedom from modulation noise, print-through and crosstalk. The independence of the quality from the medium also means that a recorder will not perform differently if different brands of tape are used, provided that they all have acceptable error rates.

★ A digital recording is no more than a series of numbers and hence can be copied through an indefinite number of generations without degradation. This implies that the life of a recording can be truly indefinite because, even if the medium begins to decay physically, the sample values can be copied to a new medium with no loss of information.

★ The use of error-correction techniques eliminates the effects of dropout. In consumer products, error correction can be used to advantage to ease the handling requirements.

★ The use of timebase correction on replay eliminates the effect of speed variations in the mechanism.

★ The use of digital recording and error correction allows the signal-to-noise ratio (SNR) of the recorded tracks to be relatively poor. The tracks can be narrow and hence achieve a saving in tape consumption when compared with an equivalent analog recorder, despite the greater bandwidth.

1.2 A short history

The shortcomings of analog processes first became obvious in computers. The accuracy of computation in analog computers was limited by component tolerance and drift, and led to the early introduction of digital computers where arbitrary accuracy could be had simply by choosing wordlengths. As a result, the digital recorder had to be developed to store the data used in computers. As the speed of execution increased, it became possible to share one processor between a number of users, provided enough rapid access storage could be found for all user programs. This led to the development of rotating drum stores, which led to the disk drive, initially with one fixed head per track, then with moving heads so that many more tracks could be accommodated at low cost. Computer tape decks could not compete with the access time of disks but offered higher density for backup, archiving and distribution. Cost per bit became one of the measurements of computer mass storage and naturally led to increases in storage density so that more data could be stored in the same size equipment.

While experiments with digitizing audio and video had proved that a desireable quality increase could be obtained, this remained academic until the cost of implementation could be compared with analog recording. Digital audio requires about one megabit per second for a single high quality signal and, as storage densities increased, digital audio suddenly became viable. The enormous consumer market for products such as Compact Disc meant that audio products took over as the state of the art in digital recording, with devices such as rotary-head digital audio tape (RDAT) offering a quantum leap in tape storage density. Whereas early digital audio recorders borrowed from computer technology, now computer technology borrows from audio in the shape of compact disc read only memory (CDROM) and digital data storage (DDS), the computer storage version of RDAT.

Recently the cost of implementing error correction at high bit rates has fallen to the point where the digital video recorder becomes viable. Broadcast video requires a data rate of around 200 megabits per second. This can be realized with lower tape consumption than the equivalent analog machine, and with the ability to copy through almost infinite generations.

Instrumentation recorders take advantage of digital technology to make the structure of the transport independent of the number of channels recorded. A number of analog channels of different bandwidth can be merged into a single digital data stream, and rotary-head recording allows high density and corresponding reduction in machine size.

1.3 Some typical machines outlined

Some outlines of typical digital machines follow to illustrate what is possible and to put the major chapters of this book into perspective.

Figure 1.3 shows some of the ways in which a digital recording can be made. Information which is originated in the digital domain, such as computer data, can enter the system directly, whereas analog inputs must pass through the sampling and quantizing processes. Once in digital form, the data are formed into blocks and the encoding section of the error-correction system supplies additional bits designed to protect the data against errors. These blocks are then converted into some form of channel code which combines the data with clock information so that it is possible to identify how many bits were recorded, even if several adjacent bits are identical. Chapter 3 deals with the extensive subject of channel coding.

The coded data are recorded on some medium, which can be optical or magnetic, disk or tape, rotary-head, moving-head or stationary head. Some media are erasable; some can only be recorded once. Chapter 2 is concerned with the recording process including recordable and erasable optical media.

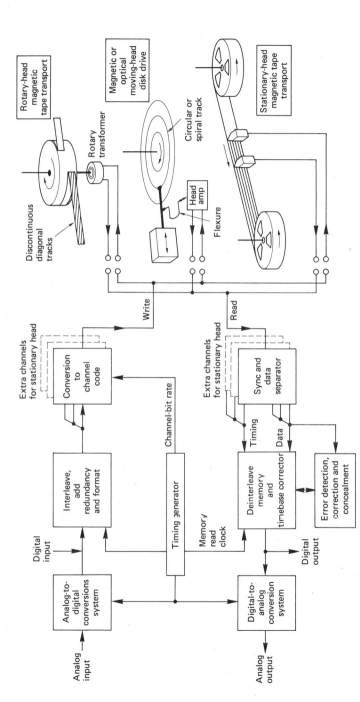

Figure 1.3 Basic digital audio recording. The essential processes in digital recording are largely independent of the kind of medium used. As shown here, data can be recorded with stationary or rotary heads, and on disk or tape. Stationary-head recorders often distribute the data from one audio channel over several tracks to reduce tape speed. the actual medium used will determine the nature of the channel-code and error-correction strategy.

Upon replaying the recording of the hypothetical machine of Figure 1.3, the errors caused by various mechanisms will be detected, corrected or concealed using the extra bits appended during the encoding process. Chapter 4 treats the subject of error correction as comprehensively as possible without becoming lost in the mathematics.

Having dealt with the theory, Chapter 5 describes a number of contrasting coding strategies used in actual formats.

1.4 Disadvantages

In this comparison of digital and analog technologies the emphasis so far has been on the advantages of digital recording. In the interests of fairness and truth we must also look at some of the problems.

1 Digital recorders must use thin tape with a fine surface finish to allow the very short wavelength recordings needed. The backcoat must be reasonably smooth to avoid damaging the recorded layer when tape is wound on the reel. This conflicts with the need for a rough backcoat to allow neat spooling at high speed. The use of short wavelengths means that all possible steps must be taken to avoid contamination. Tape has to be in cassettes, disks need to be in cartridges or, in the ultimate, in a sealed Winchester type assembly.

2 Digital channel codes are designed to restrict the range of frequencies recorded on the medium, and the playback circuits are equalized to accept these frequencies. Great difficulty is caused if a digital recording has to be played at a speed which differs from normal by more than about 10–15%. Large buffer memories can be provided to allow a variable output rate while the transport works incrementally.

2

Digital magnetic and optical recording

Although the physics of the record/replay process are unaffected by the meaning attributed to signals, the techniques used in digital recording are rather different from those found in analog recording, although the same phenomenon often shows up in a different guise. In this chapter the fundamentals of digital magnetic and optical recording are treated in sufficient depth to define the problems faced when designing a coding scheme.

2.1 Magnetic recording

In analog recording, the characteristics of the medium affect the signal recorded directly, whereas by expressing a signal in binary numerical form by sampling and quantizing, the quality becomes independent of the medium. The dynamic range required no longer directly decides the track width needed. In digital circuitry there is a great deal of noise immunity because the signal can only have two states, which are widely separated compared to the amplitude of noise. In digital magnetic recording there are also only two states of the medium N–S and S–N, but paradoxically the noise immunity is much reduced. As noise immunity is a function of track width, reduction of the working SNR of a digital track allows the same information to be carried in a smaller area of the medium, thereby improving economy of operation. It also increases the random error rate, but as an error-correction system is already necessary to deal with dropouts, it is simply made to work harder.

It is interesting to compare tape consumption between analog and digital machines where possible. A typical studio audio recorder will have 24 tracks on 2 inch tape for analog recording, whereas only ½ inch tape is necessary for digital recording of 24 or 48 tracks in the DASH format, the tape speed being roughly the same in each case. In professional video recording, the analog C-format transports 1 inch tape at 230 mm/s, whereas the D-2 composite digital recorder uses ¾ inch tape at only 130 mm/s. In digital recording narrower tracks are to be expected and steps must be taken to register the heads accurately with the tracks by appropriate mechanical design and improved edge straightness in the tape.

2.2 Head noise and head-to-tape speed

There are several important sources of replay noise in a magnetic recorder which will be examined later in this chapter. One of these is the noise from the head. All components with resistance generate noise according to their temperature, and the replay head is no exception. If a given recording exists on a tape, a better SNR will be obtained by moving the head relative to the tape at a higher speed since the head noise is constant and the signal induced is proportional to speed. This is one reason why rotary-head recorders offer better packing density than station-ary-head recorders. The other reason is much more obvious. A rotary-head machine determines track spacing by linear tape speed, whereas stationary heads are difficult to fabricate with narrow spacing between tracks. In digitizing an analog waveform there has been an exchange in the importance of SNR and bandwidth. The bandwidth of a digital channel always exceeds the bandwidth of the original analog signal, but the extra bandwidth is only required with poor SNR. This explains the paradox that greater bandwidth is needed but less tape is used. As in analog recording, the rotating head can be used to obtain high bandwidth without excessively short tape wavelengths and at moderate linear tape speed. A further advantage of rotary-head machines is that, by changing the scanner geometry, the best compromise can be reached between bandwidth and SNR. Figure 2.1 shows that, in the same area of tape, two different recordings can be made. The first has a lower

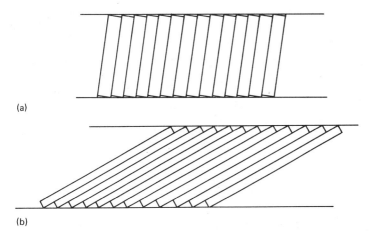

(a)

(b)

Figure 2.1 Two different rotary-head formats having the same tape consumption but different characteristics

head-to-tape speed because the tracks are shorter, but better SNR because they are wider. The second has higher bandwidth due to the longer tracks, but these tracks are narrower. In the absence of head noise, the information capacity of both formats would be the same. Where head noise is a factor the second format will be superior. The lower limit to track width is generally set by the ability to register a head with adequate precision, and sometimes track-following servos are necessary to achieve the highest densities without sacrificing the ability to interchange a recording between machines. Another technique is to use azimuth recording which gives some protection from residual tracking error. The comparison of tape consumption between RDAT and the Compact Cassette is even more dramatic because of the adoption of a rotary head with azimuth recording and track following.

Whether the machine is stationary- or rotary-head, the recorded wavelengths must be kept short to conserve tape in the direction of the track. Very short wavelengths can only be replayed with consistent intimate contact between the head and the medium, so that the surface finish of the medium must be of the highest order. The roughness of the tape backcoat must be limited to prevent the back of one layer embossing an adjacent magnetic layer when the tape is wound on a spool. Digital tape has a thin coating because thickness loss prevents flux from a thick coat being of much use at short wavelengths and because a thin coating is less prone to self-demagnetization. The thin coat needs high energy particles to allow useful replay signals with reduced magnetic volume. The backing material, or substrate, is relatively thin to allow the tape to accommodate head irregularities without losing contact, but print-through is not an issue in digital recording. A happy consequence of the use of thin tape is that more can be accomodated in a given cassette, but it does require careful transport design to avoid damage.

2.3 Basic digital magnetic recording

The basic principle of digital magnetic recording is remarkably simple. Since the medium has only two states, the record waveform will typically be a current whose direction reverses but whose magnitude remains constant, as in Figure 2.2. To provide the best SNR on replay, the current required is a little less than that needed to saturate the tape, as saturation causes fringing fields around the head and crosstalk in adjacent tracks. In recent machines the record current may be produced in an analog

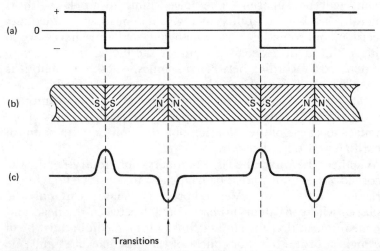

Figure 2.2 Basic digital recording. At (a) the write current in the head is reversed from time to time, leaving a binary magnetization pattern shown at (b). When replayed, the waveform at (c) results because an output is only produced when flux in the head changes. Changes are referred to as transitions

amplifier which has a response which corrects for losses in the record-head material at high frequencies. The tape encounters a strength of flux which increases and then decreases as it passes the head. The recording is actually made near the trailing pole of the head, as shown in Figure 2.3, where the flux from the head falls below the coercive force needed to change the state of the particles. The steeper the flux gradient on the trailing pole, the

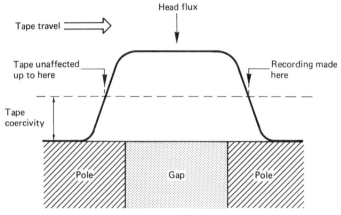

Figure 2.3 The recording is actually made near the trailing pole of the head where the head flux falls below the coercivity of the tape

shorter the wavelength which can be recorded. This is generally obtained with a relatively wide gap. Bias is unnecessary in digital recording because linearity is not a goal.

2.4 Fixed heads

The construction of a bulk ferrite multitrack head is shown in Figure 2.4, where it will be seen that space must be left between the magnetic circuits to accommodate the windings. Track spacing is improved by putting the windings on alternate sides of the gap. The parallel close-spaced magnetic circuits have considerable mutual inductance and suffer from crosstalk. This can be compensated when several adjacent tracks record together by cross-connecting antiphase feeds to the record amplifiers.

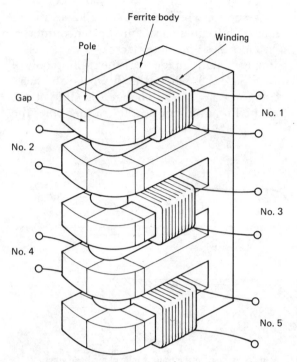

Figure 2.4 A typical bulk ferrite head. Windings are placed on alternate sides to save space, but parallel magnetic circuits have high crosstalk

Using thin-film heads, the magnetic circuits and windings are produced by deposition on a substrate at right angles to the tape plane and, as seen in Figure 2.5, they can be made very accurately at small track spacings. Perhaps more importantly, because the magnetic circuits do not have such large parallel areas, mutual inductance and crosstalk are smaller, allowing a higher practical track density.

Whereas most replay heads are inductive and generate an output which is the differential of the tape flux, there is another, less common, device known as the magneto-resistive head. In this device use is made of the Hall effect where an applied magnetic field causes electrons passing down a semiconductor to bunch together so that they experience higher resistance. The strength of flux is measured directly by the head, but it is not sensitive to polarity and it is usually necessary to incorporate a

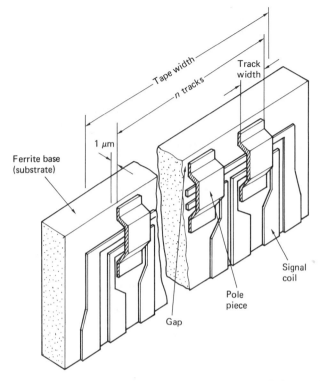

Figure 2.5 The thin-film head shown here can be produced photographically with very small dimensions. Flat structure reduces crosstalk

steady biasing field into the head so that the reversing flux from the tape is converted to a unidirectional changing flux at the sensor. Such heads have a noise advantage over inductive heads at very low tape speeds but a seperate head is required for recording.

2.5 Flying heads in disk drives

Disk drives permanently sacrifice storage density in order to offer rapid access. The use of a flying head with a deliberate air gap between it and the medium is necessary because of the high medium speed, but this causes a severe separation loss which restricts the linear density available. The air gap must be accurately maintained and, consequently, the head is of low mass and is mounted flexibly.

The aerohydrodynamic part of the head is known as the slipper; it is designed to provide lift from the boundary layer which changes rapidly with changes in flying height. It is not initially obvious that the difficulty with disk heads is not in making them fly, but in making them fly close enough to the disk surface. The boundary layer travelling at the disk surface has the same speed as the disk, but as height increases it slows down due to drag from the surrounding air. As the lift is a function of relative air speed, the closer the slipper comes to the disk the greater the lift will be. The slipper is therefore mounted at the end of a rigid cantilever sprung towards the medium. The force with which the head is pressed towards the disk by the spring is equal to the lift at the designed flying height. Because of the spring, the head may rise and fall over small warps in the disk. It would be virtually impossible to manufacture disks flat enough to dispense with this feature. As the slipper negotiates a warp it will pitch and roll in addition to rising and falling, but it must be prevented from yawing as this would cause an azimuth error. Downthrust is applied to the aerodynamic centre by a spherical thrust button, and the required degrees of freedom are supplied by a thin flexible gimbal. The slipper has to bleed away surplus air in order to approach sufficiently close to the disk, and holes or grooves are usually provided for this purpose in the same way that tyres have grooves to take away water on wet roads.

Figure 2.6 shows how disk heads are made. The magnetic circuit of disk heads was originally assembled from discrete magnetic elements. As the gap and flying height became smaller to increase linear recording density, the slipper was made from ferrite and became part of the magnetic circuit. This was completed by a small C-shaped ferrite piece which carried the coil. In thin-film heads the magnetic circuit and coil are both formed by deposition on a substrate which becomes the rear of the slipper.

In a moving-head device it is not practicable to position separate erase, record and playback heads accurately. Erase is by overwriting, and reading and writing are carried out by the same head.

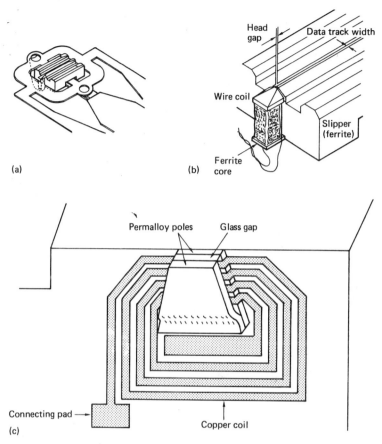

Figure 2.6 (a) Winchester head construction showing large air bleed grooves. (b) Close-up of slipper showing magnetic circuit on trailing edge. (c) Thin-film head is fabricated on the end of the slipper using microcircuit technology

2.6 Playback

When a digital recording is replayed, the output of the head will be a differentiated version of the record waveform because the head only responds to the rate of change of flux.

The initial task of the replay circuits is to reconstruct the record waveform. The amplitude of the signal is of no consequence; what matters is the time at which the write current, and hence the flux stored on the medium, reverses. This can be determined by locating the peaks of the replay impulses. At high data rates this can conveniently be done by differentiating the signal and looking for zero crossings. Figure 2.7 shows that this results in noise between the peaks. This problem is overcome by the gated peak detector, where only zero crossings from a pulse which exceeds the threshold will be counted. This method is almost universally used in disk drives,

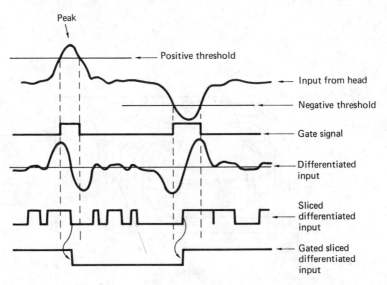

Figure 2.7 Gated peak detection rejects noise by disabling the differentiated output between transitions

whereas at the relatively low data rates of digital audio, the record waveform can also be restored by integration, which opposes the differentiation of the head, as shown in Figure 2.8 [1].

There are a number of details which must be added to this simplistic picture in order to appreciate the real position. Figure 2.9 shows that the differentiating effect of the replay process causes the head output initially to rise at 6 dB per octave from a DC response of zero. Although a high frequency recording can be made throughout the thickness of the medium, the flux deep within the medium cannot couple with the replay head at short

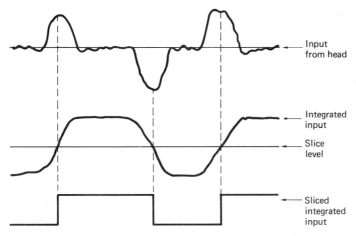

Figure 2.8 Integration method for recreating write-current waveform

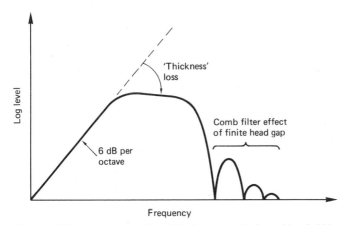

Figure 2.9 The major mechanisms defining magnetic channel bandwidth

wavelengths and so as recorded wavelength falls, a thinner and
thinner layer near the surface remains responsible for the replay
flux [2]. This is called thickness loss, although it is a form of
separation loss, and it causes a loss of 6 dB per octave which
cancels the differentiating effect to give a region of constant
frequency response. The construction of the head results in the
same action as that of a two-point transversal filter because the

two poles of the head see the tape with a small delay interposed due to the finite gap. As expected, the head response is like a comb filter with the well-known nulls where flux cancellation takes place across the gap. Clearly, the smaller the gap the shorter the wavelength of the first null. This contradicts the requirement that the record head have a large gap. In quality analog audio recorders it is the norm to have different record and replay heads for this reason, and the same is sometimes true in digital recording.

Figure 2.10 shows that when an uneven duty cycle is recorded there are a number of problems. The lack of DC response causes a level shift. Combined with the finite rate of change of voltage,

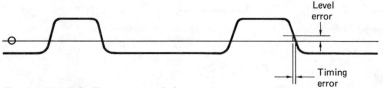

Figure 2.10 A DC offset can cause timing errors

the shift can cause timing errors unless care is taken to slice the signal about its own centre. The finite gap in the replay head causes closely spaced flux reversals to interfere with one another, which causes peak shift distortion (also known as intersymbol interference or pulse crowding) and tends to reduce the asymmetry of the waveform, again causing timing errors. The mechanism responsible for peak shift is shown in Figure 2.11(a). The results of two independent and opposite transitions passing the head are shown, and summing these gives the result of replaying two close together. Interaction between the two transitions reduces the amplitude of the signal and moves the peaks apart. Avoidance of peak shift requires equalization of the channel [3], and this can be done by a network after the replay head, termed an equalizer or pulse sharpener [4], as shown in Figure 2.11(b), or before the record head, where it is called precompensation, as shown in Figure 2.11(c). Both of these techniques use transversal filtering to oppose the inherent transversal effect of the head. By way of contrast, partial response replay takes advantage of intersymbol interference and, indeed, depends on it.

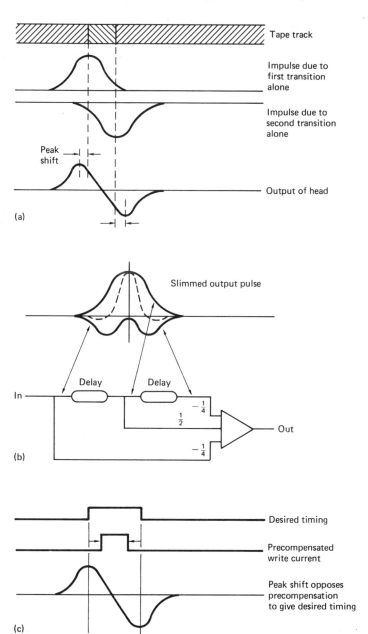

Tape track

Impulse due to
first transition
alone

Impulse due to
second transition
alone

Peak shift

Output of head

(a)

Slimmed output pulse

Delay

Delay

In

$-\frac{1}{4}$

$\frac{1}{2}$

Out

$-\frac{1}{4}$

(b)

Desired timing

Precompensated
write current

Peak shift opposes
precompensation
to give desired timing

(c)

Figure 2.11 (a) Peak shift distortion can be reduced by (b) equalization in replay, or (c) precompensation

2.7 Azimuth recording and rotary heads

Conventional magnetic recorders record the transitions on the tape track at right angles to the edge of the track, and Figure 2.12 shows that it is necessary to leave so-called guard bands between tracks to allow some tracking error without causing crosstalk from adjacent tracks. These guard bands represent wasted tape.

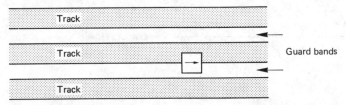

Figure 2.12 In conventional recording, a space or guard band must be left between tracks so that if a head is misaligned, the output signal simply reduces instead of becoming a composite signal from two tracks. The guard bands represent unused tape

Figure 2.13(a) shows that in azimuth recording the transitions are laid down at an angle to the track by using a head which is tilted. Machines using azimuth recording must always have an even number of heads so that adjacent tracks can be recorded with opposite azimuth angle. The two track types are usually referred to as A and B. Figure 2.13(b) shows the effect of playing a track with the wrong type of head. The playback process suffers from an enormous azimuth error, the effect of which can be understood by imagining the tape track to be made from many identical parallel strips. In the presence of azimuth error the strips at one edge of the track are played back with a phase shift relative to strips at the other side. At some wavelengths the phase shift will be 180° and there will be no output; at other wavelengths, especially long wavelengths, some output will reappear. The effect is rather like that of a comb filter and serves to attenuate crosstalk due to adjacent tracks. Since no tape is wasted between the tracks, efficient use is made of the tape. The term guard-band-less recording is often used instead of, or in addition to, the term azimuth recording. The failure of the azimuth effect at long wavelengths is a characteristic of azimuth recording, and it is necessary to ensure that the spectrum of the signal to be recorded has a small low frequency content.

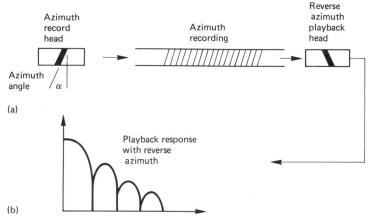

Figure 2.13 In azimuth recording (a), the head gap is tilted. If the track is played with the same head, playback is normal, but the response of the reverse azimuth head is attenuated (b)

In digital recording there is often no separate erase process and erasure is achieved by overwriting with a new waveform. When a rotary-head machine uses overwriting in conjunction with azimuth recording, the recorded tracks can be made rather narrower than the head pole simply by reducing the linear speed of the tape so that it does not advance so far between sweeps of the rotary heads. This can be seen in Figure 2.14. In RDAT the head pole is 20.4 μm wide but the tracks it records are only 13.59 μm wide. The same head can be used for replay, even

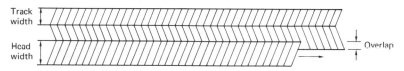

Figure 2.14 In azimuth recording, the tracks can be made narrower than the head pole by overwriting the previous track

though it is 50% wider than the tracks. It can be seen from Figure 2.15 that there will be crosstalk from tracks at both sides of the home track, but this crosstalk is attenuated by azimuth effect. The amount by which the head overlaps the adjacent track determines the spectrum of the crosstalk since it changes the delay in the azimuth comb-filtering effect. More importantly,

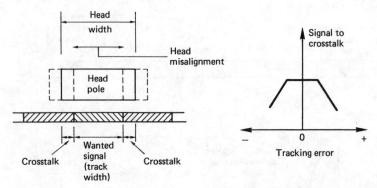

Figure 2.15 When the head pole is wider than the track, the wanted signal is picked up along with crosstalk from the adjacent tracks. If the head is misaligned, the signal-to-crosstalk ratio remains the same until the head fails to register with the whole of the wanted track

the signal-to-crosstalk ratio becomes independent of tracking error over a small range because as the head moves to one side the loss of crosstalk from one adjacent track is balanced by the increase of crosstalk from the track on the opposite side. This phenomenon allows for some loss of track straightness and for the residual error which is present in all track-following servo systems [5].

The azimuth angle used has to be chosen with some care. The greater the azimuth angle the less will be the crosstalk, but the effective writing speed is the head-to-tape speed multiplied by the cosine of the azimuth angle. A further smaller effect is that the tape is anisotropic because of particle orientation. Noise due to the medium, head or amplifier is virtually unaffected by the azimuth angle and there is no point in reducing crosstalk below the noise. The typical value of $\pm 20°$ reduces crosstalk to the same order as the noise, with a loss of only 1 dB due to the apparent reduction in writing speed.

2.8 Equalization

In practice there are difficulties in providing correct equalization at all times. Tape surface asperities and substrate irregularities cause variations in the intimacy of head contact, which changes the response at high frequencies much more than at low frequencies, thereby undermining any fixed equalization. In disk drives, the varying radius of the tracks results in a linear density variation of about two to one. The presence of the air film causes severe separation loss, and peak shift distortion is a major problem. The flying height of the head varies with the radius of the disk track, and this makes it difficult to provide accurate equalization of the replay channel. The write current is often controlled as a function of track radius so that the changing reluctance of the air gap does not change the resulting record flux. Equalization is used on recording in the form of precompensation, which moves recorded transitions in such a way as to oppose the effects of peak shift. Optimum equalization is difficult under dynamic conditions, although in principle an adaptive equalizer can be made which uses the timing errors caused by poor equalization to change the response.

In most of the above, a clearer picture has been obtained by studying the impulse response of devices than from the frequency response, and this follows from the impulsive nature of digital techniques.

2.9 Types of optical disk

The principles of laser disks will now be described, based on an introduction to optical physics.

There are numerous types of optical disk and these have different characteristics [6]. There are, however, three broad groups which can be usefuly compared:

1 The Compact Disc (CD) is an example of a read-only laser disk, which is designed for mass duplication by stamping. The Compact Disc cannot be recorded. Figure 2.16 shows that the information layer of CD is an optically flat mirror upon which microscopic bumps are raised. A thin coating of aluminium renders the layer reflective. When a small spot of light is focused on the information layer, the presence of the bumps affects the way in which the light is reflected back and variations in the reflected light are detected to read the disc. The height of the bumps in the mirror surface has to be one-quarter of the wavelength of the light used, so that light reflected from a bump has travelled half a wavelength less

than light reflected from the mirror surface and will thus be out of phase with it. This results in destructive interference in light returning to the source, and the light will escape, in any direction where constructive interference allows, as a diffraction pattern primarily along a disc radius. Effectively, a bump scatters light, thus reducing the amount of reflected light. Figure 2.16 also illustrates the very small dimensions involved. For comparison, some 60 CD tracks can be accommodated in the groove pitch of a vinyl LP. These dimensions demand the utmost cleanliness in manufacture.

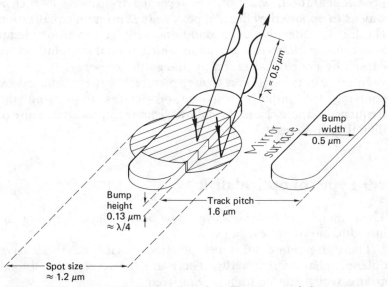

Figure 2.16 CD readout principle and dimensions. The presence of a bump causes destructive interference in the reflected light

2 Some laser disks can be recorded, but once a recording has been made it cannot be changed or erased. These are usually referred to as write-once-read-many (WORM) disks. The general principle is that the disk contains a thin layer of metal; on recording, a powerful laser melts spots on the layer. Surface tension causes a hole to form in the metal, with a thickened rim around the hole. Subsequently a low power laser can read the disk because the metal reflects light but the hole passes it through. Clearly, once a pattern of holes has been made it is permanent.

3 Erasable optical disks have essentially the same characteristic as magnetic disks in that new and different recordings can be made in the same track indefinitely, but there is usually a separate erase cycle needed before a new recording can be made since overwrite is not generally possible. To contrast with systems such as the Compact Disc, which requires considerable processing after the write stage before reading is possible, such systems are called direct-read-after-write (DRAW) disks.

2.10 Optical theory

All these technologies are restricted by the wave and quantum nature of light and depend heavily on certain optical devices such as lasers, polarizers and diffraction gratings. These subjects will be outlined here.

Wave theory of light suggests that a plane wave advances because an infinite number of point sources can be considered to emit spherical waves which will only add when they are all in the same phase. This can only occur in the plane of the wavefront. Figure 2.17 shows that at all other angles interference between spherical waves is destructive.

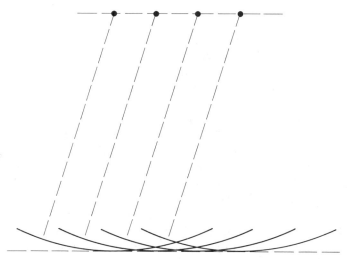

Figure 2.17 Plane-wave propagation considered as infinite numbers of spherical waves

When such a wavefront arrives at an interface with a denser medium the velocity of propagation is reduced; therefore the wavelength in the medium becomes shorter, causing the wavefront to leave the interface at a different angle (Figure 2.18).

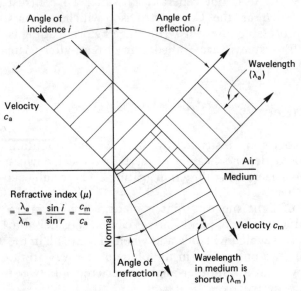

Figure 2.18 Reflection and refraction, showing the effect of the velocity of light in a medium

This is known as refraction. The ratio of velocity *in vacuo* to velocity in the medium is known as the refractive index of that medium; it determines the relationship between the angles of the incident and refracted wavefronts. Reflected light, however, leaves at the same angle to the normal as the incident light. If the speed of light in the medium varies with wavelength, incident white light will be split into a rainbow spectrum leaving the interface at different angles. Glass used for chandeliers and cut glass is chosen for this property, whereas glass for optical instrument will be chosen to have a refractive index which is as constant as possible with changing wavelength.

When a wavefront reaches an aperture which is small compared to the wavelength, the aperture acts as a point source and the process of diffraction can be observed as a spherical wavefront leaving the aperture, as shown in Figure 2.19. Where

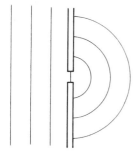

Figure 2.19 Diffraction as a plane wave reaches a small aperture

the wavefront passes through a regular structure, known as a diffraction grating, light on the far side will form new wavefronts wherever radiation is in phase, and Figure 2.20 shows that these will be at an angle to the normal depending on the spacing of the structure and the wavelength of the light. A diffraction grating illuminated by white light will produce a rainbow spectrum at each side of the normal. To obtain a fixed angle of diffraction, monochromatic light is necessary.

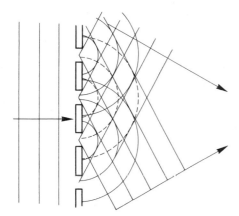

Figure 2.20 In a diffraction grating, constructive interference can take place at more than one angle for a single wavelength

For a given wavelength, the greater the spatial frequency of the grating (bars per unit of distance) the greater will be the angle of diffraction. A corollary of this effect is that the more finely detailed an object is the greater the angle over which light must be collected to see the detail. The light-collecting angle of a lens shown in Figure 2.21 is measured by the numerical aperture (NA), which is the sine of the angle between the optical axis and the wavefront carrying the finest detail in the image. All lenses thus act as spatial filters which cut off at a spatial frequency limited by NA. The response is known as the modulation

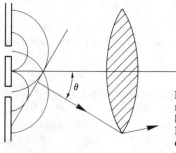

Figure 2.21 Fine detail in an object can only be resolved if the diffracted wavefront due to the highest spatial frequency is collected by the lens. Numerical aperture (NA) = sin θ, and as θ is the diffraction angle it follows that, for a given wavelength, NA determines resolution

transfer function (MTF). Light travelling on the axis of a lens is conveying the average brightness of the image and not the detail which is conveyed in the more oblique light collected at the rim of the lens. Lenses can fall short of their theoretical MTF due to shortcomings in manufacture. If a lens is made accurately enough, a wavefront which has passed through it will have the same phase over its entire area. Where wavefront aberrations have a variance of less than the square of the wavelength divided by 180, the lens is said to meet the Maréchal criterion, which essentially means that the performance of the lens is as good as it is going to get because it is now diffraction-limited rather than tolerance-limited.

When a diffraction-limited lens is used to focus a point source on a plane the image will not be a point owing to exclusion of the higher spatial frequencies by the finite numerical aperture. The resulting image is in fact the spatial equivalent of the impulse response of a low pass filter, and results in a diffraction pattern known as an Airy pattern, after Sir George Airy who first quantified the intensity function. It is the dimensions of the Airy pattern which limit the density of all optical media since it controls the minimum size of features that the laser can produce or resolve. The only way a laser disk could hold more data would be if the working wavelength could be reduced since this would reduce the size of the spot.

By the same argument, it is not much use trying to measure the pit dimensions of a laser disk with an optical microscope. It is necessary to use an electron microscope to make measurements where conventional optics are diffraction-limiting.

2.11 The laser

The semiconductor laser is a relative of the light-emitting diode (LED). Both operate by raising the energy of electrons to move them from one valence band to another conduction band. Electrons which fall back to the valence band emit a quantum of energy as a photon whose frequency is proportional to the energy difference between the bands. The process is described by Planck's law:

Energy difference $E = h \times f$

where h = Planck's constant

$= 6.6262 \times 10^{-34}$ joules

For gallium arsenide the energy difference is about 1.6 eV, where 1 eV is 1.6×10^{-19} joules. Using Planck's law, the frequency of emission will be

$$f = \frac{1.6 \times 1.6 \times 10^{-19}}{6.6262 \times 10^{-34}} \text{ Hz}$$

The wavelength will be c/f where

c = the velocity of light = 3×10^8 m/s

$$\text{Wavelength} = \frac{3 \times 10^8 \times 6.6262 \times 10^{-34}}{2.56 \times 10^{-19}} \text{ m}$$

$= 780$ nanometres

In the LED, electrons fall back to the valence band randomly and the light produced is incoherent. In the laser, the ends of the semiconductor are optically flat mirrors which produce an optically resonant cavity. One photon can bounce to and fro, exciting others in synchronism, to produce coherent light. This can result in a runaway condition where all available energy is used up in one flash. In injection lasers, an equilibrium is reached between energy input and light output, allowing continuous operation. The equilibrium is delicate and such devices are usually fed from a current source. To avoid runaway when temperature change disturbs the equilibrium, a photosensor is often fed back to the current source. Such lasers have a finite life and become steadily less efficient. The feedback will maintain output and it is possible to anticipate the failure of the laser by monitoring the drive voltage needed to give the correct output.

2.12 Polarization

In natural light, the electric-field component will be in many planes. Light is said to be polarized when the electric-field direction is constrained. The wave can be considered as made up from two orthogonal components. When these are in phase the polarization is said to be linear. When there is a phase shift between the components the polarization is said to be elliptical, with a special case at 90° called circular polarization. These types of polarization are contrasted in Figure 2.22.

To create polarized light, anisotropic materials are convenient. Polaroid material, invented by Edwin Land, is vinyl which is made anisotropic by stretching it while hot. This causes the long polymer molecules to line up along the axis of

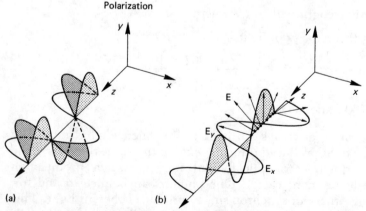

Figure 2.22 (a) Linear polarization: orthogonal components are in phase. (b) Circular polarization: orthogonal components are in phase quadrature

stretching. If the material is soaked in iodine the molecules are rendered conductive and short out any electric-field component along themselves. Electric fields at right angles are unaffected; thus the transmission plane is at right angles to the stretching axis.

Stretching plastics can also result in anisotropy of refractive index; this effect is known as birefringence. If a linearly polarized wavefront enters such a medium the two orthogonal components propagate at different velocities causing a relative phase difference proportional to the distance travelled. The plane of polarization of the light is rotated. Where the thickness of the material is such that a 90° phase change is caused, the device is known as a quarter-wave plate. The action of such a device is shown in Figure 2.23. If the plane of polarization of the incident light is at 45° to the planes of greatest and least refractive index, the two orthogonal components of the light will be of equal magnitude and this results in circular polarization. Similarly, circular-polarized light can be returned to the linear-polarized state by a further quarter-wave plate. Rotation of the plane of polarization is a useful method of separating incident and reflected light in a laser pickup. Using a quarter-wave plate, the

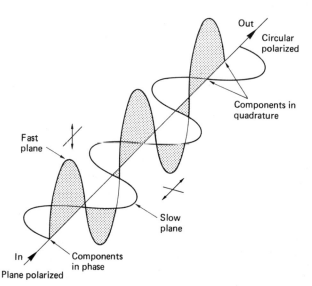

Figure 2.23 Different speed of light in different planes rotates the plane of polarization in a quarter-wave plate to give a circular-polarized output

plane of polarization of light leaving the pickup will have been turned 45°, and on return it will be rotated a further 45° so that it is now at right angles to the plane of polarization of light from the source. The two can easily be separated by a polarizing prism, which acts as a transparent block to light in one plane but as a prism to light in the other plane.

2.13 Thermomagneto-optics

A relatively recent and fascinating field is the use of magneto-optics [7], also known more fully as thermomagneto-optics, for data storage where the medium can be rerecorded.

Writing in a DRAW device makes use of a thermomagnetic property posessed by all magnetic materials, which is that above a certain temperature, known as the Curie temperature, their coercive force becomes zero. This means that they become magnetically very soft, and take on the flux direction of any externally applied field. On cooling, this field orientation will be frozen in the material and the coercivity will oppose attempts to change it. Although many materials possess this property there are relatively few which have a suitably low Curie temperature. Compounds of terbium and gadolinium have been used, and one of the major problems to be overcome is that almost all materials that are suitable from a magnetic viewpoint corrode very quickly in air.

Figure 2.24 shows how a DRAW disk is written. If the disk is considered to be initially magnetized along its axis of rotation with the north pole upwards, it is rotated in a field of the opposite sense which is produced by coils and which is weaker than the room-temperature coercivity of the medium. The coils will therefore have no effect. A laser beam is focused on the medium as it turns, and a pulse from the laser will momentarily heat a very small area of the medium past its Curie temperature, whereby it will take on a reversed flux due to the presence of the field coils. This reversed-flux direction will be retained indefinitely as the medium cools. The storage medium is thus clearly magnetic, but the writing mechanism is the heat produced by light from a laser; hence the term thermomagneto-optics. The advantage of this writing mechanism is that there is no physical contact between the writing head and the medium.

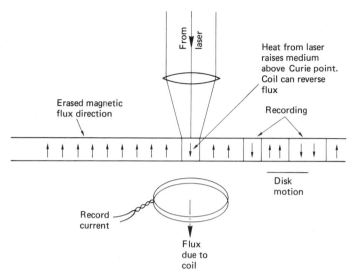

Figure 2.24 The thermomagneto-optical disk uses the heat from a laser to allow magnetic field to record on the disk

The distance can be several millimetres, some of which is taken up with a protective layer to prevent corrosion. In prototypes this layer is glass but it is expected that commercially available DRAW disks will be plastic.

The laser beam will supply a relatively high power for writing because it is supplying heat energy. For reading, the laser power is reduced such that it cannot heat the medium past the Curie temperature, and it is left on continuously. Readout depends on the so-called Kerr effect, or the related Faraday effect, both of which are a rotation of the plane of polarization of light due to a magnetic field. The name of the effect depends on whether transmitted or reflected light is of interest. The magnetic areas written on the disc will rotate the plane of polarization of incident polarized light to two different planes and it is possible to detect the change in rotation by passing the reflected light through a further polarizing screen. The light whose plane of polarization is more nearly parallel with the transmission plane of the screen will pass more easily than the light whose plane of polarization is rotated away from the transmission plane, and a photosensor will detect an intensity change which recreates the write waveform. The readout signal is very small since the Kerr effect is subtle. The plane of polarization is rotated only a fraction of a degree in typical devices, which makes the replay signal prone to noise. In order to change a recording it must first be erased. The laser is set to the power level required for writing but the coils adjacent to the disk are fed with a reversed current to that used in the write process. As the laser scans the old recording, the heat raises the track above its Curie temperature and causes it to take on the direction of the applied field, which is that of the erased state. The coil current is then set back to the write direction and the disk track can be rewritten with laser pulses as before. The erase process is necessary because the write process can only set the magnetic state. It cannot reset it.

Experimental recordable Compact Discs have been made based on this principle [8,9].

2.14 Optical readout

The information layer of an optical disc is read through the thickness of the disc. Figure 2.25 shows that this approach causes the readout beam to enter and leave the disc surface through the largest possible area. The actual dimensions of CD are shown in the diagram. Despite the minute spot size of about 1.2 μm diameter, light enters and leaves through a 0.7 mm-diameter circle. As a result, surface debris has to be three orders of magnitude larger than the readout spot before the beam is obscured. The size of the entry circle is a function of the refractive index of the disc material, the numerical aperture of the objective lens, and the thickness of the disc. The method of readout through the disc thickness tolerates surface scratches very well. By way of contrast, the label side of CD is actually more vulnerable than the readout side because the lacquer coating is only 30 μm thick. The Compact Disc is unique in being single sided. Most optical disks are in fact made from two disks sandwiched together with the two information layers on the inside.

Continuing the example of CD, the specified wavelength of 780 nm and the numerical aperture of 0.45 results in an Airy function where the half-power level is at a diameter of about 1 μm. The first dark ring will be at about 1.9 μm diameter. As the illumination follows an intensity function it is really

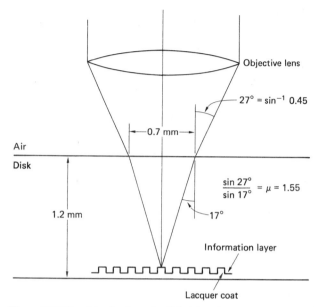

Figure 2.25 The objective lens of a CD pickup has a numerical aperture (NA) of 0.45; thus the outermost rays will be inclined at approximately 27° to the normal. Refraction at the air/disk interface changes this to approximately 17° within the disk. Thus light focused to a spot on the information layer has entered the disk through a 0.7 mm diameter circle, giving good resistance to surface contamination

meaningless to talk about spot size unless the relative power level is specified. The analogy is quoting frequency response without dB limits.

Allowable crosstalk between tracks then determines the track pitch. The first ring outside the central disc carries some 7% of the total power and limits crosstalk performance. The track spacing is such that with a slightly defocused beam and a slight tracking error, crosstalk due to adjacent tracks is acceptable. Since aberrations in the objective will increase the spot size and crosstalk, the CD specification requires the lens to be within the Maréchal criterion. Clearly, the numerical aperture of the lens, the wavelength of the laser, the refractive index and thickness of the disc, and the height and size of the bumps must all be simultaneously specified.

The cutter spot size determines the reader spot size, and this in turn determines the shortest wavelength along the track which can be resolved. If the track velocity is specified, the wavelength limit becomes a frequency limit. The optical cutoff frequency is that frequency where the amplitude of modulation replayed from the disc has fallen to zero, and it is given by

$$F_c = \frac{2NA}{\text{wavelength}} \times \text{velocity}$$

The minimum linear velocity of CD is 1.2 m/s, giving a cutoff frequency of

$$F_c = \frac{2 \times 0.45 \times 1.2}{780 \times 10^{-9}} = 1.38\,\text{MHz}$$

Figure 2.26 shows that the frequency response falls linearly to the cutoff and that actual measurements are only a little worse than the theory predicts. Clearly, to obtain any noise immunity the maximum operating frequency must be rather less than the cutoff frequency. The maximum frequency used in CD is 720 kHz, which represents an absolute minimum wavelength of 1.666 μm, or a bump length of 0.833 μm, for the lowest permissible track speed of 1.2 m/s used on the full-length 75 min playing discs. One hour playing discs have a minimum bump length of 0.972 μm at a track velocity of 1.4 m/s. The maximum frequency is the same in both cases.

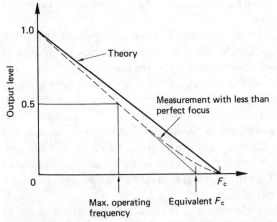

Figure 2.26 Frequency response of laser pickup. Maximum operating frequency is about half of cutoff frequency F_c

2.15 Structure of laser drive

A typical laser disk drive resembles a magnetic drive in that it has a spindle drive mechanism to revolve the disk and a positioner to give radial access across the disk surface. The pickup must contain a dynamic focusing mechanism to follow disk warps and it must be able to keep the laser spot on track despite runout in the disk. The positioner has to carry a collection of lasers, lenses, prisms, gratings, and so on, and usually cannot be accelerated as fast as a magnetic-drive positioner. A penalty of the very small track pitch possible in laser disks, which gives the enormous storage capacity, is that very accurate track following is needed and it takes some time to lock on to a track. For this reason tracks on laser disks are usually made as a continuous spiral, rather than the concentric rings of magnetic disks. In this way a continuous data transfer involves no more than track-following once the beginning of the file is located.

References

1. DEELEY, E.M. (1986) Integrating and differentiating channels in digital tape recording. *Radio Electron. Eng.*, **56** 169–173
2. MEE, C.D. (1978) *The Physics of Magnetic Recording.*, Amsterdam and New York: Elsevier–North Holland Publishing
3. JACOBY, G.V. (1975) Signal equalization in digital magnetic recording. *IEEE Trans. Magn.*, **11**, 302–305
4. SCHNEIDER, R.C. (1975) An improved pulse-slimming method for magnetic recording. *IEEE Trans. Magn.*, **11**, 1240–1241
5. ARAI, T., NOGUCHI, T., KOBAYASHI, M. and OKAMOTO, H. (1986) Digital signal processing technology for R-DAT. *IEEE Trans. Consum. Electron.*, **CE–32**, 416–424
6. DOUWHUIS, G. *et al* (1985) *Principles of Optical Disc Systems*. Bristol: Adam Hilger
7. OHR, S. (1985) Magneto-optics combines erasability and high-density storage. *Electronic Design* (11 July) 93–100
8. SCHOUHAMER IMMINK, K.A. and BRAAT, J.J.M. (1983) Experiments towards an erasable Compact Disc digital audio system. Presented at 73rd Audio Engineering Society Convention (Eindhoven, 1983), preprint 1970(E2)
9. KURAHASHI, A. *et al.* (1985) Development of an erasable magneto-optical digital audio recorder. Presented at 79th Audio Engineering Society Convention (New York, 1985), preprint 2296(A-1)

3

Channel coding

Chapter 2 outlined the basic physics of various recording processes and introduced numerous shortcomings and restrictions from which real recording channels will suffer. In this chapter these shortcomings will be categorized and coding methods to overcome them will be described.

3.1 Shortcomings of recording channels

Noise in the channel causes uncertainty about the voltage of the reproduced signal. Jitter causes uncertainty about the time at which a particular event occurred. The frequency response of the channel then places an overall limit on the spacing of events in the channel. Particular emphasis must be placed on the interplay of bandwidth, jitter, and noise, which will be shown here to be the key to the design of a successful channel code.

In laser recording, the interference readout process will respond down to DC, but usually the low frequency portion of the channel is required by the focus and tracking mechanisms, and DC-free channel codes will still be necessary. The high frequency response is governed by the modulation transfer function of the optics which is normally limited by the numerical aperture of the objective. The frequency response of a laser recorder falls to zero at the cutoff frequency and, unlike magnetic recording, never rises again.

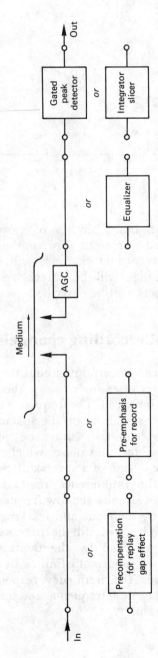

Figure 3.1 A general recording channel showing the various processes described in the text. The system shown here permits recording of a binary waveform

3.2 Jitter windows

Figure 3.1 shows several possibilities for a complete digital recording channel. The reconstituted waveform at the output of this channel will now be a replica of the timing of the record signal, with the addition of time uncertainty in the position of the edges due to noise, jitter, and dubious equalization. In the same way that binary circuits reject noise by using two voltage levels which are spaced further apart than the uncertainty due to noise, digital recording combats time uncertainty by using events, known as transitions, at multiples of some basic time period which is larger than the typical time uncertainty. Figure 3.2 shows how this jitter-rejection mechanism works.

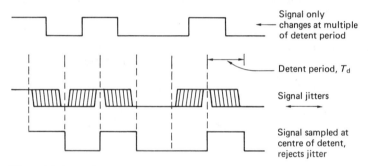

Figure 3.2 A certain amount of jitter can be rejected by changing the signal at multiples of the basic detent period T_d

As digital transitions occur at multiples of a basic period, an oscilloscope, which is triggered on random data, will show an eye pattern if connected to the output of the equalizer. Study of the eye pattern reveals how well the coding used suits the channel [1]. Noise closes the eyes in a vertical direction and jitter closes the eyes in a horizontal direction, as shown in Figure 3.3. In the centre of the eyes, at regular intervals, the receiver must make binary decisions about the state of the signal, high or low. If the eyes remain sensibly open, this will be possible. Clearly, more jitter can be tolerated if there is less noise, and vice versa. Information theory usually only takes account of SNR and bandwidth when assessing channel capacity. Magnetic and optical recorder channels will never achieve these capacities because of jitter.

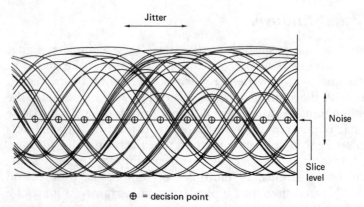

Figure 3.3 At the decision points, the receiver must make binary decisions about the voltage of the signal, whether it is above or below the slicing level. If the eyes remain open, this will be possible in the presence of noise and jitter

It is not possible to record data directly onto the medium because in real data continuous ones and continuous zeros can occur and, as shown in Figure 3.4, this is effectively a DC component of the source data. Alternate ones and zeros represent the other extreme, a frequency of half the bit rate, which is known as the Nyquist rate. Magnetic recorders will not

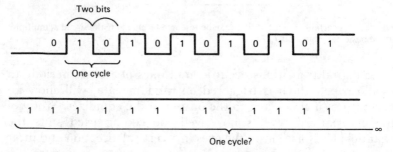

Figure 3.4 The extreme cases of real data. Alternate ones and zeros gives the highest or Nyquist rate (= half bit rate). Continuous ones (or zeros) gives DC. Real data fill the spectrum from DC to Nyquist rate

respond to DC, nor is it possible to discriminate between successive identical bits in a channel subject to time instability.

Both these problems can be solved with a suitable channel code, which will combine a clock with the data prior to recording, in a way which reduces the DC content and permits separation of adjacent symbols on replay. Figure 3.5 shows that a channel coder is necessary prior to the record stage and that a decoder, known as a data separator, is necessary after the replay stage.

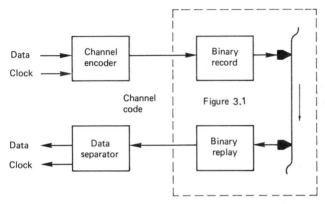

Figure 3.5 In channel coding, the input data and clock are combined into a single waveform called the channel code. On replay the channel code is restored to the original data stream by the data separator

Some codes eliminate DC content entirely, which is advantageous for rotary-head recording. Some codes can reduce the channel bandwidth needed by lowering the upper spectrum limit. This permits higher linear density, but usually at the expense of jitter rejection. A code with a narrow spectrum has a number of advantages. The reduction in asymmetry will reduce peak shift and data separators can lock more readily where the possible frequencies are fewer. In theory, the narrower the spectrum the less noise, but excessive noise filtering can ruin the equalization and thus nullify any gain.

A convenient definition of a channel code (for there are certainly others) is: 'A method of modulating real data such that they can be reliably received despite shortcomings of a real channel, while making maximum economic use of the channel capacity.'

The storage density of data recorders has steadily increased due to improvements in medium and transducer technology, but modern storage densities are also a function of improvements in channel coding. Figure 3.6(a) shows how linear density improvements due to channel coding alone have occurred, and

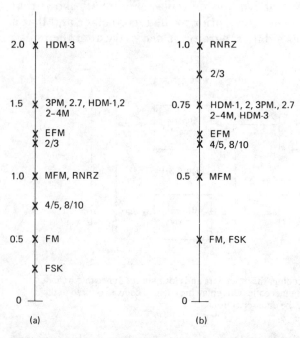

(a)   (b)

Figure 3.6 (a) Comparison of codes by density ratio; (b) comparison of codes by figure of merit. Note how 4/5, 2/3, 8/10 + RNRZ move up because of good jitter performance; HDM-3 moves down because of jitter sensitivity

introduces one of the fundamental parameters of a channel code, the density ratio (DR). One definition of density ratio is that it is the worst-case ratio of the number of data bits recorded to the number of transitions in the channel. It can also be thought of as the ratio between the Nyquist rate of the data and the frequency response of the channel. When better hardware is available to increase the capacity of a channel, the use of a higher density-ratio code multiplies the capacity further. It should be appreciated that many of the codes described in this chapter are protected by patents and that non-optimal codes are often devised to avoid the need to pay royalties on a patented code.

The basic time periods of the recorded signal are called positions or detents, in which the recorded flux will be reversed or stay the same according to the state of a channel bit which describes the detent. The symbol used for the units of channel time is T_d. Channel coding is the art of converting real data into channel bits. It is important to appreciate that the convention in coding is that a channel bit one represents a flux change, whereas a zero represents no change. This is confusing because the input data only change where successive bits differ. The differentiating action of magnetic playback has a lot to do with these conventions.

As jitter is such an important issue in digital recording, a parameter has been introduced to quantify the ability of a channel code to reject time instability. This parameter, the jitter margin, also known as the window margin or phase margin (T_w), is defined as the permitted range of time over which a transition can still be received correctly, divided by the data bit-cell period (T).

Since equalization is often difficult in practice, a code which has a large jitter margin will sometimes be used with short recorded wavelengths because it resists the effects of peak shift distortion. Such a code may achieve a working density better than a code with a higher density ratio but poor jitter performance.

A more realistic comparison of code performance will be obtained by taking into account both density ratio and jitter margin. This is the purpose of the figure of merit (FoM), which is defined as DR × T_w. Figure 3.6(b) shows a comparison of codes by FoM.

3.3 Simple codes

Some actual codes will now be examined.

The essence of channel coding is to convert real data into channel bits. Since the time quantizing is linear, channel codes lend themselves to convenient comparison by analysis of the autocorrelation function. In autocorrelation a signal is delayed and multiplied by itself. When the delay is swept, a graph is obtained of the product versus delay, known as the autocorrelation function. Most of the parameters of a code can be read from the autocorrelation function at a glance, whereas the more common use of the code spectrum makes this more difficult. Figure 3.7 shows the autocorrelation functions of a number of codes.

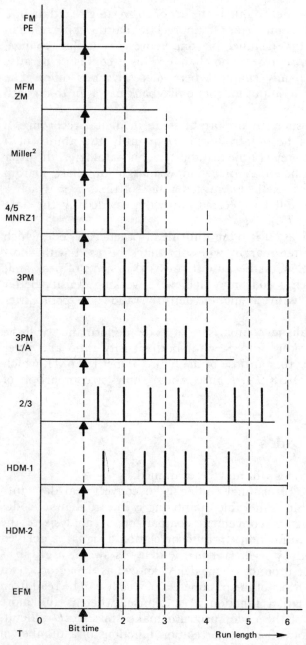

Figure 3.7 Comparison of codes by autocorrelation function of run length

The adoption of FM in analog recorders permitted the recording of DC levels for instrumentation and video. When a binary signal is fed to a frequency modulator, the result is frequency shift keying (FSK) shown in Figure 3.8(a). This is inherently DC-free and suits radio transmission and rotary-head recorders. It is used on the master recorders for production of CD, and indeed with any VCR used with a digital audio PCM adaptor. Frequency shift keying has a poor density ratio, but this was unimportant in PCM adaptors because the bandwidth of the VCR is more than adequate.

The limiting case of FSK is binary FM (also known as Manchester code) shown in Figure 3.8(b). This was the first practical self-clocking binary code. It is DC-free and very easy to encode and decode. It remains in use today where recording density is not of prime importance, for example in single-density floppy disks, in SMPTE/EBU time code for professional audio and video recorders and the reference track in DASH format. It is also specified for the AES/EBU digital audio interconnect standard which transmits audio serially down cables.

In FM there is always a transition at the bit-cell boundary which acts as a clock. For a data one, there is an additional

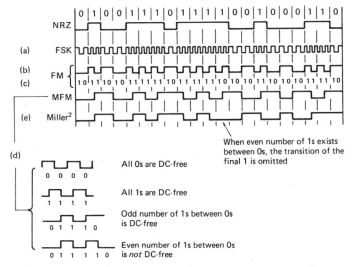

Figure 3.8 Evolution from FSK to Miller^2. Note that although Miller^2 is DC-free T_{max} and L_c are worse than MFM

transition at the bit-cell centre. Figure 3.8(c) shows that each data bit is represented by two channel bits. For a data zero, they will be 10, and for a data one they will be 11. Since the first bit is always one, it conveys no information, and is responsible for the density ratio of only one half. Since there can be two transitions for each data bit, the jitter margin can only be half a bit, and the FoM resulting is only 0.25. The high clock content of FM does, however, mean that data recovery is possible over a wide range of speeds; hence the use for timecode.

In MFM the highly redundant clock content of FM was reduced by the use of a phase-locked loop in the receiver which could flywheel over missing clock transitions. This technique is implicit in all the more advanced codes. The bit-cell centre transition on a data one was retained, but the bit-cell boundary transition is now only required between successive zeros. There are still two channel bits for every data bit, but adjacent channel bits will never be one, doubling the minimum time between transitions, and giving a DR of 1. Clearly, the coding of the current bit is now influenced by the preceding bit. The maximum number of prior bits which affect the current bit is known as the constraint length L_c, measured in data-bit periods. For MFM $L_c = T$. Another way of considering the constraint length is that it assesses the number of data bits which may be corrupted if the receiver misplaces one transition. If L_c is long, all errors will be burst errors.

MFM doubled the density ratio compared to FM without changing the jitter performance; thus the FoM also doubled. It was adopted for many rigid disks at the time of its development and remains in use on double-density floppy disks. It is not, however, DC-free. Figure 3.8(d) shows how MFM can have DC content, and that in Miller^2 code the DC content is eliminated by a slight increase in complexity. Wherever an even number of ones occurs between zeros the transition at the last one is omitted. This creates an additional entry in the autocorrelation function because T_{max} has increased. Miller^2 code was used in some early stationary-head digital audio recorders and is currently in use in high-bit-rate instrumentation recording, and in the D-2 composite digital video cassette for professional use [2,3].

A similar performance is given by zero modulation, but with an increase in complexity [4].

3.4 Group codes

Further improvements in coding rely on converting patterns of real data to patterns of channel bits with more desirable characteristics, using a conversion table known as a codebook. If a data symbol of m bits is considered, it can have 2^m different combinations. As it is intended to discard undesirable patterns to improve the code, it follows that the number of channel bits n must be greater than m. The number of patterns which can be discarded is

$$2^n - 2^m$$

One name for the principle is group code recording (GCR), and an important parameter is the code rate, defined as

$$\text{Code rate, } R = \frac{m}{n}$$

It will be evident that the jitter margin T_w is numerically equal to the code rate and thus a code rate close to unity is desirable. The choice of patterns used in the codebook will be those which give the desired balance between clock content, bandwidth, and DC content.

Figure 3.9 shows that the upper spectral limit can be made to be some fraction of the channel bit rate according to the minimum distance between ones in the channel bits. This is known as T_{min}, also referred to as the minimum transition parameter M, and in both cases is measured in data bits T. It can be obtained by multiplying the number of channel detent

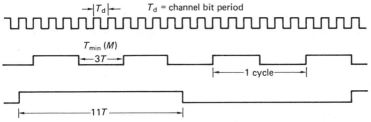

Figure 3.9 A channel code can control its spectrum by placing limits on $T_{min}(M)$ and T_{max} which define upper and lower frequencies. Ratio of T_{max}/T_{min} determines asymmetry of waveform and predicts DC content and peak shift. Example shown is EFM

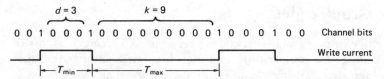

Figure 3.10 Channel-bit convention is that a 1 represents a transition. Parameters *d* and *k* are the number of zeros between ones. *d*= min, *k*=max. Clearly T_{min}, T_{max} are greater than *d*, *k* by one channel-bit period

periods between transitions by the code rate. Unfortunately, codes are measured by the number of consecutive zeros in the channel bits given the symbol *d*, which Figure 3.10 shows is always one less than the number of detent periods. In fact T_{min} is numerically equal to the density ratio:

$$T_{min} = M = DR = \frac{(d + 1) \times m}{n}$$

It will be evident that choosing a low code rate could increase the density ratio, but it will impair the jitter margin. The figure of merit is

$$FoM = DR \times T_w = \frac{(d + 1) \times m^2}{n^2}$$

since $T_w = \dfrac{m}{n}$

Figure 3.9 also shows that the lower spectral limit is influenced by the maximum distance between transitions T_{max}. This is also obtained by multiplying the maximum number of detent periods between transitions by the code rate. Again, codes are measured by the maximum number of zeros between channel ones, *k*, and thus

$$T_{max} = \frac{(k + 1) \times m}{n}$$

and the maximum/minimum ratio *P* is:

$$P = \frac{k + 1}{d + 1}$$

The length of time between channel transitions is known as the run length. Another name for this class is the run-length-limited (RLL) codes [5]. Since *m* data bits are considered as one symbol, the constraint length L_c will be increased in RLL codes to at least *m*. It is, however, possible for a code to have run-length limits without it being a group code.

In practice, the junction of two adjacent channel symbols may violate run-length limits, and it is necessary to create a further codebook of symbol size *2n* which converts violating codes to acceptable codes. This is known as merging and follows the golden rule that the substitute *2n* symbol must finish with a pattern which eliminates the possibility of a subsequent violation. These patterns must also differ from all other symbols.

Substitution may also be used to different degrees in the same nominal code to allow a choice of maximum run length, e.g. 3PM [6]. The maximum number of symbols involved in a substitution is denoted by *r* [7,8]. There are many RLL codes and the parameters *d,k,m,n* and *r* are a way of comparing them.

Sometimes the code rate forms the name of the code, as in 2/3, 8/10 and eight-to-fourteen modulation (EFM); at other times the code may be named after the *d,k* parameters, as in 2,7 code.

Various examples will be given which illustrate the principles involved.

4/5 code uses 16 out of 32 possible channel symbols to represent the data. The criterion for 4/5 was high clock content to give immunity to jitter without a great sacrifice of DR [9]. The codebook is shown in Table 3.1. Each one in the code represents a flux reversal, and there are never more than three channel bits (2.4 data bits) of time between clock edges ($k = 2$). This permits a simple automatic game control (AGC) system to be used in the read circuits. As codes had to be rejected to achieve the main criterion, the remaining codes have to be accepted; thus the minimum run length is only one bit since adjacent ones are allowed in the code book ($d = 0$). The code is thus described as 0,1,4,5,1. $L_c = 4T$, and the density ratio is given by

$$DR = \frac{(d + 1) \times m}{n} = 0.8$$

The spectrum needed is thus 1.25 times that of the data, but there can be no merging violations, and an extremely good window margin T_w of $0.8\,T$ is obtained, giving an FoM of 0.64.

Table 3.1 The codebook of 4/5 code. Maximum number of zeros (k) is two; thus T_{max} is $4(k + 1)/5 = 2.4$ bits. Adjacent ones are permitted: thus DR = 4/5

Decimal	Data Binary	Channel bits
0	0000	11001
1	0001	11011
2	0010	10010
3	0011	10011
4	0100	11101
5	0101	10101
6	0110	10110
7	0111	10111
8	1000	11010
9	1001	01001
10	1010	01010
11	1011	01011
12	1100	11110
13	1101	01101
14	1110	01110
15	1111	01111

This code was used by the IBM 6250 BPI tape format and represented an improvement factor of nearly four over the 1600 BPI phase-encoded (PE) system which preceded it. The FoM was better than PE by a factor of more than 2½, thus reducing the improvements needed to the head and tape.

Figure 3.11(a) shows an optimized code which also illustrates the process of merging. This is a 1,7,2,3,2 code known as 2/3. It is designed to have a large window to resist peak shift in disk drives, along with a good density ratio [10]. In 2/3 code, pairs of data bits create symbols of three adjacent channel bits. For bandwidth reduction all codes with adjacent ones are eliminated. This halves the code spectrum and the density ratio improves accordingly

$$DR = \frac{(d + 1) \times m}{n} = \frac{2 \times 2}{3} = 1.33$$

In Figure 3.11(b) the effect of some data combinations will be code violations. Thus pairs of three channel-bit symbols are replaced with a new six channel-bit symbol; L_c is thus $4\,T$, the same as for 4/5 code. The jitter window is given by

$$T_w = \frac{m}{n} = \frac{2}{3}\,T$$

Data	Code
0 0	1 0 1
0 1	1 0 0
1 0	0 0 1
1 1	0 1 0

(a)

Data	Illegal code	Substitution
0 0 0 0	1 0 1 1 0 1	1 0 1 0 0 0
0 0 0 1	1 0 1 1 0 0	1 0 0 0 0 0
1 0 0 0	0 0 1 1 0 1	0 0 1 0 0 0
1 0 0 1	0 0 1 1 0 0	0 1 0 0 0 0

(b)

Figure 3.11 2/3 code. At (a) two data bits (m) are expressed as three channel bits (n) without adjacent transitions ($d=1$). Violations are dealt with by substitution

$$\text{DR} = \frac{(d+1)m}{n} = \frac{2 \times 2}{3} = 1.33$$

Adjacent data pairs can break the encoding rule; in these cases substitutions are made, as shown at (b)

and the FoM is

$$\frac{2}{3} \times \frac{4}{3} = \frac{8}{9}$$

This is an extremely good figure for an RLL code and is some 10% better than the FoM of 3PM [11] and 2,7.

Figure 3.12 shows an 8,14 code (EFM) used in the Compact Disc. Here eight-bit symbols are represented by 14-bit channel symbols [12]. There are 256 combinations of eight data bits, whereas 14 bits have 16K combinations. Of these, only 267 satisfy the criteria that the maximum run length shall not exceed 11 channel bits ($k = 10$) nor be less than three channel bits ($d = 2$). A section of the codebook is shown in the diagram. In fact 258 codes of the 267 possible codes are used because two

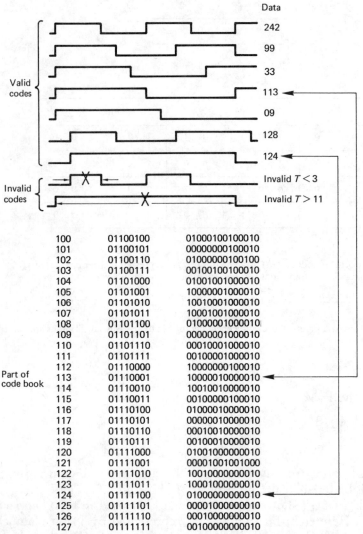

100	01100100	01000100100010
101	01100101	00000000100010
102	01100110	01000000100100
103	01100111	00100100100010
104	01101000	01001001000010
105	01101001	10000001000010
106	01101010	10010001000010
107	01101011	10001001000010
108	01101100	01000001000010
109	01101101	00000001000010
110	01101110	00010001000010
111	01101111	00100001000010
112	01110000	10000000100010
113	01110001	10000010000010
114	01110010	10010010000010
115	01110011	00100001000010
116	01110100	01000010000010
117	01110101	00000010000010
118	01110110	00010010000010
119	01110111	00100010000010
120	01111000	01001000000010
121	01111001	00001001001000
122	01111010	10010000000010
123	01111011	10001000000010
124	01111100	01000000000010
125	01111101	00001000000010
126	01111110	00010000000010
127	01111111	00100000000010

Figure 3.12 EFM code: $d=2$, $k=10$. Eight data bits produce 14 channel bits plus three packing bits. Code rate is 8/17. $DR=(3 \times 8)/17 = 1.41$

unique synchronizing patterns are used to denote the beginning of a subcode block. It is not possible to prevent violations between adjacent channel symbols by substitution, and three extra merging bits are necessary between symbols. These bits are used for the additional task of DC control because the CD channel code must be DC-free. The packing bits are selected by computing the digital sum value (DSV) of the channel bits. The DSV is calculated by adding one to account for every channel-bit period during which the code waveform is high, and by subtracting one for every period during which it is low. Figure 3.13 shows that if two successive channel symbols have the same sense of DC content, they can be made to cancel one another by placing an extra transition in the packing bits, which has the effect of inverting the second pattern and reversing its DC content. The DC-free code can be high pass filtered on replay, and the lower frequency signals are then used by the focus and tracking servos without noise due to the DC content of the modulation. Encoding EFM is complex but this is acceptable because there are relatively few CD cutters made. Decoding is simpler and can be done with a lookup table. The relationship between the data patterns and channel bits was computer-optimized to permit the implementation of a programmable logic array (PLA) decoder with minimum complexity.

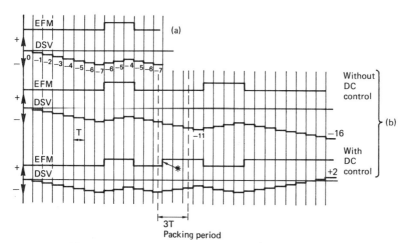

Figure 3.13 (a) Digital sum value example calculated from EFM waveform. (b) Two successive 14T symbols without DC control (upper) give DSV of −16. Additional transition (*) results in DSV of +2, anticipating negative content of next symbol

Owing to the inclusion of the merging bits, the code rate becomes 8/17 and the density ratio becomes

$$\frac{3 \times 8}{17} = 1.41$$

and the FoM is

$$\frac{3 \times 8^2}{17^2} = 0.66$$

The code is thus a $2,10,8,17,r$ system, where r only has meaning in the context of DC control [13]. The constraints d and k can still be met with $r = 1$ because of the merging bits.

The figure of merit is less useful for optical media because the rigid, non-contact medium is largely jitter-free. The density ratio and freedom from DC are the most important factors here.

A different approach to merging is taken by the 4/6M code used in multitrack ProDigi format recorders. As will be seen from Table 3.2, the input data group will be either four bits or eight bits, depending on the data pattern, and will be encoded into six or nine channel bits. In some channel patterns, the first channel bit will be the opposite of the last channel bit of the previous group. As there are never two adjacent ones in the

Table 3.2 The 4/6M code of ProDigi multitrack recorders. Four or six data bits become six or nine channel bits. X represents 1 if the end of previous group is zero and vice versa

Data	Channel bits	Data	Channel bits
0000	010000	0100	010010
000100	X00010001	0101	X00100
000101	X00100001	0110	010100
000110	X01000001	0111	X01000
000111	X01010001	1000	X01001
001000	010000001	1001	010001
001001	010010001	1010	X00010
001010	010100001	1011	X01010
001011	X00010000	1100	X00000
001100	X01010000	1101	X00001
001101	010010000	1110	X00101
001110	X00100000	1111	010101
001111	010100000		

channel patterns, T_{min} is 1.33 T_d and thus the density ratio is also 1.33. As the code rate is 4/6, the jitter window T_w is 0.66. The FoM becomes 0.89, which is the same as that of 2/3.

The low tape consumption of RDAT is achieved by a combination of narrow track-spacing and high linear data density along the track. The latter is achieved by a combination of head design and the channel code used [14]. The head gap used is typically 0.25 μm.

The essential feature of the channel code of RDAT is that it must be able to work well in an azimuth recording system. There are many channel codes available but few of them are suitable for azimuth recording because of the large amount of crosstalk. The crosstalk cancellation of azimuth recording fails at low frequencies, so a suitable channel code must not only be free of DC, it must also suppress low frequencies. A further issue is that erasure is by overwriting, and as the heads are optimized for short-wavelength working, best erasure will be when the ratio between the longest and shortest wavelengths in the recording is small.

In Table 3.3 some examples from the 8/10 group code of RDAT are shown. Clearly, a channel waveform which spends as much time high as low has no net DC content and so all ten bit-patterns which meet this criterion of zero disparity can be found. As adjacent channel ones are permitted, the window margin and DR will be 0.8, giving an FoM of 0.64. This is the

Table 3.3 Some of the 8/10 codebook for non-zero DSV symbols (two entries) and zero DSV symbols (one entry)

Eight-bit dataword	Ten-bit codeword	DSV	Alternative codeword	DSV
00010000	1101010010	0		
00010001	0100010010	2	1100010010	− 2
00010010	0101010010	0		
00010011	0101110010	0		
00010100	1101110001	2	0101110001	− 2
00010101	1101110011	2	0101110011	− 2
00010110	1101110110	2	0101110110	− 2
00010111	1101110010	0		

same as the IBM 4/5 code, but by using larger symbols more combinations are available for optimization. Unfortunately there are not enough DC-free combinations in ten channel bits to provide the 256 patterns necessary to record eight data bits. A further constraint is that it is desirable to restrict the maximum run length to improve overwrite capability and reduce peak shift. In the 8/10 code of RDAT, no more than three channel zeros are permitted between channel ones, which makes T_{max} only four times T_{min}. There are only 153 ten-bit patterns which are within this maximum run length and which have a DSV of zero.

The remaining 103 data combinations are recorded using channel patterns that have non-zero DSV. Two channel patterns are allocated to each of the 103 data patterns. One of these has a DSV of $+2$; the other has a DSV of -2. For simplicity, the only difference between them is that the first channel bit is inverted. The choice of which channel-bit pattern to use is based on the DSV due to the previous code.

For example, if several bytes have been recorded with some of the 153 DC-free patterns, the DSV of the code will be zero. The first data byte is then found which has no zero disparity pattern. If the $+2$ DSV pattern is used, the code at the end of the pattern will also become $+2$ DSV. When the next pattern of this kind is found, the code having DSV of -2 will automatically be selected to return the channel DSV to zero. In this way the code is kept DC-free but the maximum distance between transitions can be shortened. A code of this kind is known as a low disparity code.

In order to reduce the complexity of encoding logic it is usual in GCR to computer-optimize the relationship between data patterns and code patterns. This has been done for 8/10 so that the conversion can be performed in a programmed logic array. Only DC-free or DSV $= +2$ patterns are produced by the logic since the DSV $= -2$ pattern can be obtained by reversing the first bit. The assessment of DSV is performed in an interesting manner. If in a pair of channel bits the second bit is one, the pair must be DC-free because each detent has a different value. If the five even channel bits in a ten-bit pattern are checked for parity and the result is one, the pattern could have DSV of 0, ±4 or ±8. If the result is zero, the DSV could be ±2, ±6 or ±10. However, the codes used are known to be either zero or $+2$ DSV so the state of the parity bit discriminates between them.

Figure 3.14(a) shows the truth table of the PLA, and Figure 3.14(b) shows the encoding circuit. The lower set of XOR gates calculate parity on the latest pattern to be recorded, and store the DSV bit in the latch. The next data byte to be recorded is fed to the PLA, which outputs a ten-bit pattern. If this is a zero disparity code, it passes to the output unchanged. If it is a DSV = + 2 code, this will be detected by the upper XOR gates. If the latch is set, this means that a previous pattern was + 2 DSV, and so the first bit of the channel pattern is inverted by the XOR gate in that line, and the latch will be cleared because the DSV of the code has been returned to zero.

Decoding is simpler because there is a direct relationship between ten-bit codes and eight-bit data.

3.5 Tracking signals

Rotary-head digital audio tape uses a track-following system where certain areas of the track are set aside for alignment patterns. It is, however, possible to bury low frequency tracking tones within digital data. A group code is used, where for each data group several valid channel groups exist, each having a different DC content. By choosing a group not only from the data to be recorded but also to produce the desired DC level, it is possible to generate a low frequency from the sequence of DC levels used. This can be filtered from the data frequencies used.

3.6 Convolutional RLL codes

It has been mentioned that a code can be run-length limited without being a group code. An example of this is HDM-1 code which is used in DASH format (digital audio stationary head) recorders. The coding is best described as convolutional and is rather complex, as Figure 3.15 shows [15]. The DR of 1.5 is achieved by treating the input bit pattern of 0,1 as a single symbol which has a transition recorded at the centre of the one. The code then depends upon whether the code continues with ones or reverts to zeros. The shorter run-lengths are used to describe sequential ones; the longer run-lengths describe sequential zeros up to a maximum run-length of 4.5 T with a

$$a = A + CZ + Y \,(\overline{C} \oplus \overline{F} \,(G + H))$$

$$b = A \,(B + D\overline{E}) + \overline{A} \,(\overline{B} + \overline{C})$$

$$c = \overline{A}C + A \,(\overline{D} + E) + BDE$$

$$d = A \,(C + BD\overline{E}) + CDE + \overline{C}Z + (\overline{A}\,\overline{B} \oplus \overline{F}\,\overline{G}HY)$$

$$\overline{e} = (AB + \overline{D}) \,\overline{E} + \overline{A}\,\overline{B}CDE + Y\overline{F} \,(\overline{G} + \overline{H})$$

$$f = \overline{A}\,\overline{E} \,[C + (B \oplus D)] + [(\overline{D} + C\overline{E}) \oplus F \,(\overline{G} + \overline{H})]$$

$$\overline{g} = \overline{F}\,\overline{G} + Y + (B + C) \,Z$$

$$h = FG\overline{H} + \overline{F}\,\overline{Y}$$

$$i = H + FG + \overline{F}\,Y \qquad \text{where } Y = \overline{A} \,(\overline{B} + C) \,D\overline{E}$$

$$j = F\overline{G} + \overline{F}\,\overline{Y} \qquad\qquad\quad\; Z = \overline{A}\,\overline{D}\,\overline{E}\,F \,(\overline{G} + \overline{H})$$

(a)

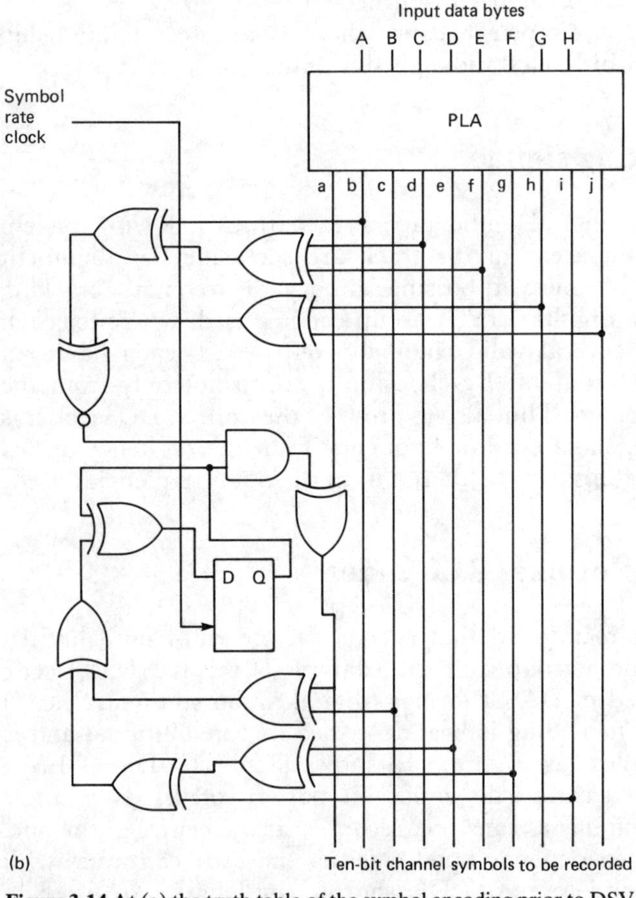

(b)

Figure 3.14 At (a) the truth table of the symbol encoding prior to DSV control. At (b) this circuit controls code disparity by remembering non-zero DSV in the latch and selecting a subsequent symbol with opposite DSV

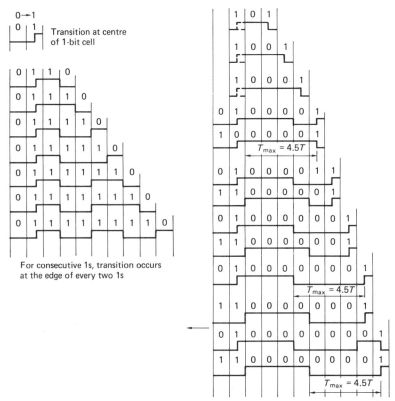

Figure 3.15 HDM-1 code of the DASH format is encoded according to the above rules. Transitions will never be closer than 1.5 bits, nor further apart than 4.5 bits

constraint length of 5.5 T. In HDM-2, a derivative of HDM-1, the maximum run-length is reduced to 4 T with the penalty that L_c becomes 7.5 T.

The 2/4M code used by the Mitsubishi ProDigi ¼ inch format recorders [16] is also convolutional and has an identical density ratio and window margin to HDM-1; T_{max} is eight bits. Neither HDM-1 nor 2/4M claim to be DC-free but this is of less consequence in stationary heads, where linear density is of greater importance. Encoding of 2/4M is just as devious as HDM-1 and is shown in Figure 3.16. Two data bits form a group and result in four channel bits where there are always two channel zeros between ones, to obtain T_{min} of 1.5. However, there are numerous exceptions to the coding to prevent

X X X X E4 E3 E2 E1 D D L1 L2 L3 L4 X X X X

Running sample of
ten data bits

DD = current set of data bits
E(N) = earlier data bits
(a)   L(N) = later data bits

Data bits DD	Channel bits C_1 C_2 C_3 C_4	Exceptions and substitutions
00	0 1 0 0 0 0 0 0 0 0 0 1	E4 E3 = 10 E4 E3 ≠ 10 and E2 E1 = 10 and L1 L2 ≠ 01 E4 E3 ≠ 10 and E2 E1 = 10 and L1 L2 = 01
01	0 0 1 0	
10	Y 0 0 1 0 1 0 0 0 0 0 1 0 0 0 0	E2 E1 ≠ 10 and L1 L2 = 00 E2 E1 = 10 and L1 L2 = 10 and L3 L4 = 00 E2 E1 = 10 and L1 L2 = 00 E2 E1 = 10 and L1 L2 = 10 and L3 L4 = 00
11	Y 0 0 0	

(b) ,   Y = XNOR of C_3 C_4 of previous DD

Figure 3.16 Coding rules for 2/4 M code. At (a) a running sample is made of two data bits DD and earlier and later bits. At (b) two data bits become the four channel bits shown except when the substitutions specified are made

run-length violations, which require examination of a running sample of ten data bits; this is why the code has to be described as a convolutional rather than a substituting group code.

3.7 Randomized NRZ

Genuine data are unsuitable for direct recording because, as has been seen, they have an undefined maximum run length, T_{max}, which poses severe problems with clock recovery, AGC, and DC content. In other respects, however, raw data has potential because the density ratio of unity is combined with the extremely good jitter window, which is also unity, to give an FoM of 1, which is higher than the best group codes.

It is possible to convert raw data into a channel code in a non-redundant fashion by performing a modulo-2 (XOR) addition with a pseudo-random sequence. As Figure 3.17 shows, the result of this process is that T_{max} is drastically reduced.

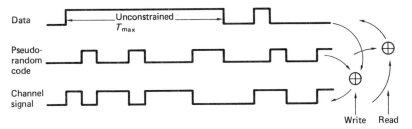

Figure 3.17 Modulo-2 addition with a pseudo-random code removes unconstrained runs in real data. Identical process must be provided on replay

Obviously the same pseudo-random sequence must be provided on replay, synchronized to the data, if there is to be correct recovery. In practice the system cannot accept truly random data, since if by chance the data are identical to the pseudo-random sequence, the system breaks down. The probability of such an occurrence is low and the error-correction system would deal with it. The so-called randomized NRZI coding has been used in D-1 component digital video recorders and in the Ampex DCRSi instrumentation recorder because the pseudo-random sequence reduces the DC content of the waveform, which is essential as both formats require a rotary transformer in the channel.

3.8 Partial response

It has been stated that the head acts as a transversal filter because it has two poles. In addition the output is differentiated so that the head may be thought of as a $(1 - D)$ impulse response system where D is the delay which is a function of the tape speed and gap size. It is this delay which results in intersymbol interference. Conventional equalizers attempt to oppose this effect, and succeed in raising the noise level in the process of making the frequency response linear. Figure 3.18 shows that the frequency response necessary to pass data with insignificant peak shift is a bandwidth of half the bit rate, which is the Nyquist rate. In Class IV partial response, the frequency response of the system is made to have nulls at DC and at the Nyquist rate. This is achieved by an overall impulse response of

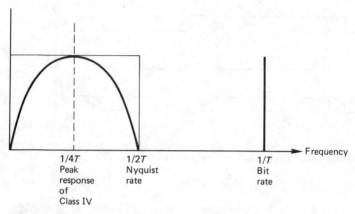

Figure 3.18 Class IV response has spectral nulls at DC and the Nyquist rate, giving a noise advantage, since magnetic replay signal is weak at both frequencies in a high density channel

$(1 - D^2)$ where D is now the bit period. There are a number of ways in which this can be done.

If the head gap is made equal to one bit the $(1 - D)$ head response may be converted to the desired response by the use of a $(1 + D)$ filter, as shown in Figure 3.19(a) [17]. Alternatively, a head of unspecified gap width may be connected to an integrator and equalized flat to reproduce the record current waveform before being fed to a $(1 - D^2)$ filter, as shown in Figure 3.19(b) [18].

The result of both these techniques is a ternary signal. The eye pattern has two sets of eyes, as shown in Figure 3.19(c) [19]. When slicing such a signal, a smaller amount of noise will cause an error than in the binary case.

The treatment of the signal thus far represents an equalization technique, and not a channel code. However, to take full advantage of Class IV partial response, suitable precoding is necessary prior to recording, which does then constitute a channel-coding technique. This precoding is shown in Figure 3.20(a). Data are added modulo-2 to themselves with a two-bit delay. The effect of this precoding is that the outer levels of the ternary signals, which represent data ones, alternate in polarity on all odd bits and on all even bits. This is because the precoder acts like two interleaved one-bit delay circuits, as shown in Figure 3.20(b). As this alternation of polarity is a form of

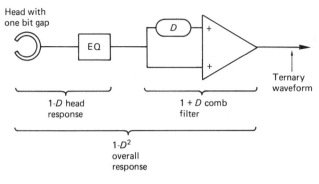

(a)

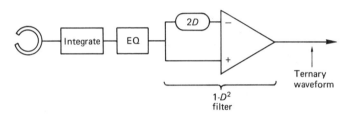

(b)

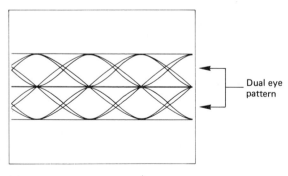

(c)

Figure 3.19 (a), (b) Two ways of obtaining partial response. (c) Characteristic eye pattern of ternary signal

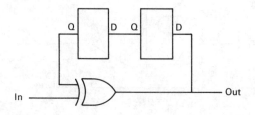

(a)

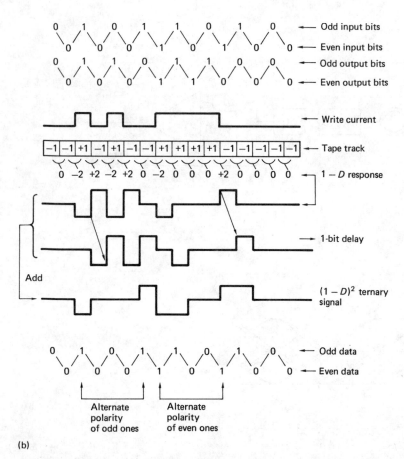

(b)

Figure 3.20 Class IV precoding at (a) causes redundancy in replay signal as derived in (b)

redundancy it can be used to recover the 3 dB SNR loss encountered in slicing a ternary eye pattern. Viterbi decoding can be used for this purpose [20]. In Viterbi decoding, each channel bit is not sliced individually; the slicing decision is made in the context of adjacent decisions. Figure 3.21 shows a replay waveform which is so noisy that at the decision point the signal voltage crosses the centre of the eye, and the slicer alone cannot tell whether the correct decision is an inner or an outer level. In this case the decoder essentially allows both decisions to stand in order to see what happens. A symbol representing indecision is output. It will be seen from the diagram that as subsequent bits are received one of these decisions will result in an absurd situation, which indicates that the other decision was the right one. The decoder can then locate the undecided symbol and set it to the correct value.

Clearly, a ternary signal having a dual eye pattern is more sensitive than a binary signal and it is important to keep the

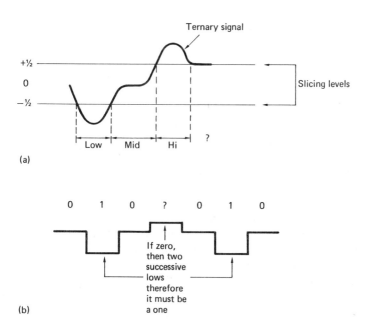

Figure 3.21 (a) A ternary signal suffers a noise penalty because there are two slicing levels. (b) The redundancy is used to determine the bit value in the presence of noise. Here the pulse height has been reduced to make it ambiguous 1/0, but only 1 is valid as 0 violates the redundancy rules

maximum run length T_{max} small in order to have accurate AGC. The use of pseudo-random coding along with partial response equalization and precoding is a logical combination [21].

Another way of using the information content of a ternary signal is to have the three states determine the amount by which a multilevel parameter changes from one channel bit to the next. A chart of this parameter versus channel symbols is called a trellis, as shown in Figure 3.22. In trellis coding, the record signal is precoded so that only certain paths through the trellis are valid, and others must represent errors which can be corrected by deducing the most likely path from the received path [22]. There is then no distinction between the channel code and the error-correction system. Viterbi decoding and trellis coding are primarily applicable to channels with random errors due to Gaussian statistics; they cannot cope with burst errors. In a head-noise-limited system, however, the use of a Viterbi detector could increase the power of an error-correction system by relieving it of the need to correct random errors due to noise. The error-correction system could then concentrate unimpaired on correcting burst errors. The significance of this statement will become clearer upon referring to Chapter 4.

3.9 Graceful degradation

In all the channel codes described here all the data bits have equal significance, and if the characteristics of the channel degrade, the probability of reception of all bits falls equally rapidly. In digital audio and video all the bits are not of equal significance since an error in the least significant bit (LSB) of a sample might pass unnoticed, whereas a most significant bit (MSB) error would be intolerable. For applications where the bandwidth of the channel is unpredictable, or where it may improve as a particular technology is mastered, a different form of channel coding has been proposed where the probability of reception of bits is not equal [23]. The channel spectrum is divided in such a way that the most significant bits of a sample occupy the lowest frequencies and the least significant bits occupy the highest frequencies.

When the channel bandwidth of such a signal is reduced, the eye pattern is affected such that some eyes become

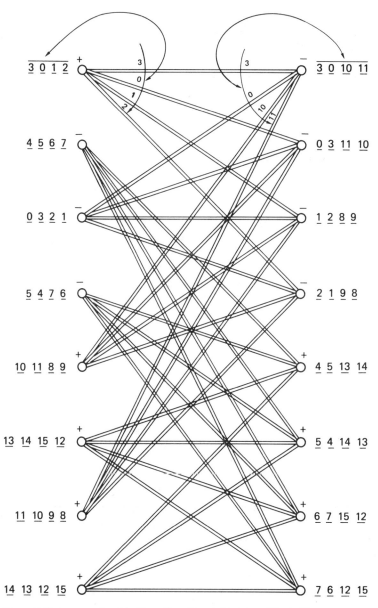

Figure 3.22 An example of trellis coding. The eight states of the trellis represent a three-bit symbol ($2^3 = 8$). From any starting state, there are four possible destinations according to a four-bit (0–15) symbol from the channel

indeterminate, but others remain sensibly open at regular intervals, guaranteeing reception of clocking and high order bits. The effect is that low order bits are in error. In a stream of audio samples this means that the waveform is sensibly the same but suffers from an increased noise level.

The error-correction techniques needed will be different in that codewords must be assembled from bits in different samples which have the same significance.

3.10 Synchronizing

In most of the codes described here an improvement in some desired parameter has been obtained either by a sacrifice of some other parameter or by an increase in complexity. Often it is the clock content which suffers, so that the number of channel bits which have to be measured between transitions becomes quite large. The only way in which the channel code can be decoded is to use a phase-locked loop to regenerate the channel-bit clock. A fixed-frequency clock would be of no use since, even if the medium could be made to move at the right speed for the channel-bit rate to match the clock rate, the instantaneous errors due to jitter would be insuperable. In phase-locked loops (PLL) the voltage-controlled oscillator is driven by a phase error measured between the output and some reference such that the oscillator eventually runs at the same frequency as the reference. If a divider is placed between the VCO and the phase comparator, as in Figure 3.23, the VCO frequency can be made to be a multiple of the reference. This also has the effect of making the loop more heavily damped. If a channel code is used as a reference to a PLL the loop will be able to make a phase comparison whenever a transition arrives, but when there are channel zeros between transitions the loop will flywheel at the last-known frequency and phase until it can rephase at a subsequent transition. In this way, cycles of the VCO can be counted to measure the number of channel zeros between transitions and hence to decode the information. Figure 3.24 illustrates this mechanism.

Clearly, data cannot be separated if the PLL is not locked, but it cannot be locked until it has seen transitions for a reasonable period. The solution is to precede each data block with a pattern

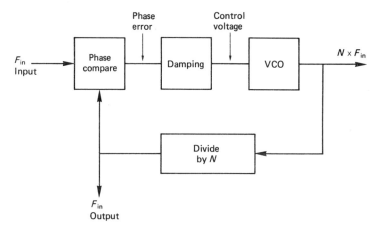

Figure 3.23 A typical phase-locked loop where the VCO is forced to run at a multiple of the input frequency. If the input ceases, the output will continue for a time at the same frequency until it drifts

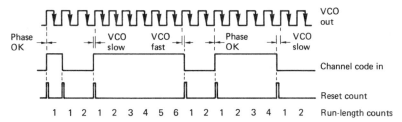

Figure 3.24 In order to reconstruct the channel patterns, a phase-locked loop is fed with the channel code, and freewheels between transitions, correcting its phase at each one. Counting the VCO edges (↓) between transitions reconstructs the channel bits. If the medium changes speed, the VCO will track. If the maximum run length is too long, the VCO will not be able to phase correct often enough, and may miscount channel bits in the presence of jitter

of transitions whose sole purpose is to provide a timing reference for synchronizing the phase-locked loop. This pattern is known as a preamble. In MFM the preamble will usually be the result of encoding all zeros, which is a square wave at the bit rate. In high density recording, the preamble may be some simple fraction of the bit rate to avoid the attenuation of the highest frequencies when the PLL is attempting to lock. In magnetic recording there is almost always a postamble at the end of the data block. Again, a few zeros are recorded after the real data.

When magnetic heads are turned off at the end of a write there is often a transient which corrupts the last bits written. The postamble can be damaged in this way without consequence. Another reason for a postamble is to enable a block to be read backwards. This is often done in computer magtapes to shorten access time. Time code has to be legible in either direction and at varying speeds. Some channel codes are designed to work backwards, such as phase encoding, 4/5GCR, zero modulation and FM. For reverse reading, the postamble will be the same length as the preamble; otherwise it will be much shorter.

Once the PLL has locked to the preamble a data stream and a clock will emerge from the data separator. It is then vital to know at what point in the data stream the preamble finishes and the actual data commences. In serial recording, words are recorded one after the other, one bit at a time with no spaces in between, so that although the designer knows that a block contains, say, 12 words of 16 bits each, the medium simply holds 192 bits in a row. If the exact position of the first bit is not known, then it is not possible to put all the bits in the right places in the right words. The effect of sync slippage is devastating because a one-bit disparity between the data-bit count and the bit stream will corrupt every word in the block, which is just as bad as a massive dropout[24].

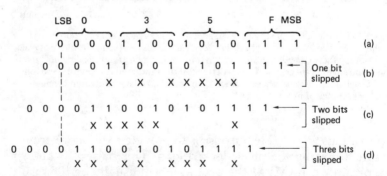

Figure 3.25 A synchronizing pattern having a low autocorrelation is shown here at (a). In (b), the pattern is one bit from synchronization and fails to match in seven places (shown as X). In (c) the pattern is two bits away from synchronization, and fails to match in six places. At (d) the pattern is three bits away from synchronization, and fails in eight places.

Owing to the large number of differences when the pattern shifts, there is a much reduced probability of an error reading the pattern causing false synchronization. The pattern shown is used in the D-1 format DVTR for both audio and video data blocks

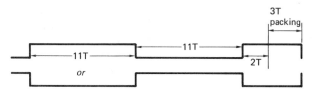

Two sequential runs of 11T cannot arise in coded data
T = Channel bit period

(a)

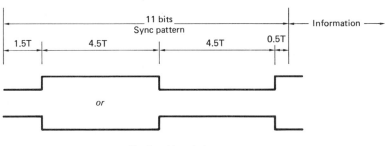

T = Data bit period

(b)

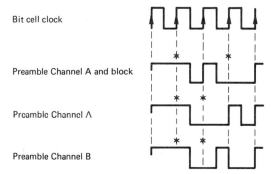

FM code must have a clock edge in every bit cell

∗ Code violation points

(c)

Figure 3.26 Sync patterns in various applications. At (a) the sync pattern of CD violates EFM coding rules, and is uniquely identifiable. At (b) the sync pattern of DASH stays within run length of HDM-1. At (c) the sync patterns of AES/EBU interconnect

The synchronization of the data separator and the synchronization to the block format are two distinct problems and they are often solved separately. At the end of the preamble a so-called sync pattern may be inserted. This is a pattern which is identical for every block; it will be recognized by the replay circuitry and used to reset the bit count through the block. By counting bits from the sync pattern and dividing by the wordlength, the replay circuitry will be able to determine the position of the boundaries between words. The sync pattern must be chosen with care so that a bit or bits in error do not cause sync to be recognized in the wrong place. Such a pattern is designed to be as different as possible to itself however many places it is shifted, which is the same as saying it has a low autocorrelation. A good example of a low autocorrelation sync pattern is that used in the D-1 format DVTR, which is 3OF5 hex, or 0000110010101111. Figure 3.25 shows how many differences are caused for different false sync states, which helps to ensure that only the correct timing is recognized. The ProDigi format uses a similar technique, except that the synchronization pattern is a pattern of channel bits not data bits.

In group codes and run-length-limited codes it is possible to combine the function of preamble and sync pattern by producing a transition pattern at the start of the block which contains timing to phase the channel bit rate PLL, but which contains run lengths which violate the limits. There is no way that these run lengths will be interpreted as data, but they can be detected by the replay circuitry. Such techniques are used in DASH format, Compact Disc, and the AES/EBU digital audio interconnect; they are illustrated in Figure 3.26.

Where reading in both directions is required a reverse sync pattern will be placed between the data and the postamble. In timecode the sync pattern is asymmetrical so that the read circuitry can tell which way the tape is moving without any other source of information.

References

1. NAKAJIMA, H. *et al.* (1983) *Digital Audio Technology*, pp.150–152. Blue Ridge Summit, Pa.: TAB Books
2. MALLINSON, J.C. and MILLER, J.W. (1977) Optimum codes for digital magnetic recording. *Radio and Electron. Eng.*, **47**, 172–176

3. MILLER, J.W. (1977) DC-free encoding for data transmission system. US Patent 4 027 335

4. PATEL, A.M. (1975) Zero-modulation encoding in magnetic recording. *IBM J. Res. Dev.*, **19**, 366–378

5. TANG, D.T. (1969) Run-length-limited codes. IEEE International Symposium on Information Theory

6. COHN, M. and JACOBY, G. (1982) Run-length reduction of 3PM code via lookahead technique. *IEEE Trans. Magn.*, **18**, 1253–1255

7. HORIGUCHI, T. and MORITA, K. (1976) On optimisation of modulation codes in digital recording. *IEEE Trans. Magn.*, **12**, 740–742

8. FRANASZEK, P.A. (1970) Sequence state methods for run-length limited coding. *IBM J. Res. Dev.* **14**, 376–383

9. TAMURA, T. *et al.* (1972) A coding method in digital magnetic recording. *IEEE Trans. Magn.*, **8**, 612–614

10. JACOBY, G.V. and KOST, R. (1984) Binary two-thirds-rate code with full word lookahead. *IEEE Trans. Magn.*, **20**, 709–714

11. JACOBY, G.V. (1977) A new lookahead code for increased data density. *IEEE Trans. Magn.*, **13**, 1202–1204

12. OGAWA, H. and SCHOUHAMER IMMINK, K.A. (1982) EFM – the modulation method for the Compact Disc digital audio system. In *Digital Audio*, edited by B. Blesser, B. Locanthi and T.G. Stockham Jr, pp.117–124. New York: Audio Engineering Society

13. SCHOUHAMER IMMINK, K.A. and GROSS, U. (1983) Optimization of low-frequency properties of eight to fourteen modulation. *Radio Electron. Eng.*, **53**, 63–66

14. FUKUDA, S., KOJIMA, Y., SHIMPUKU, Y. and ODAKA, K. (1986) 8/10 modulation codes for digital magnetic recording. *IEEE Trans. Magn.* **22**, 1194–1196

15. DOI, T.T. (1983) Channel codings for digital audio recordings. *J. Audio Eng. Soc.* **31**, 224–238

16. ANON., P.D. (1986) format for stationary head type 2-channel digital audio recorder. Mitsubishi (January)

17. YOKOYAMA, K. (1982) Digital video tape recorder. *NHK Technical Monograph*, No. 31 (March)

18. COLEMAN, C.H. *et al.* (1985) High data-rate magnetic recording in a single channel. *J.IERE*, **55**, 229–236

19. KOBAYASHI, H. (1970) Application of partial-response channel coding to magnetic recording systems. *IBM J. Res. Dev.*, **14**, 368–375

20. FORNEY, G.D. JR (1973) The Viterbi algorithm. *Proc. IEEE*, **61**, 268–278

21. WOOD, R.W. and PETERSEN, D.A. (1986) Viterbi detection of class IV partial response on a magnetic recording channel. *IEEE Trans. Commum.* **34**, 454–461

22. WOLF, J.K. and UNGERBOECK, G. (1900) Trellis coding for partial response channels. Center for Magnetic Recording Research, University of California, San Diego

23. SCHOUHAMER IMMINK, K.A. (1987) Graceful degradation of digital audio transmission systems. Presented at 82nd Audio Engineering Society Convention (London, 1987) preprint 2434(C-3)

24. GRIFFITHS, F.A. (1980) A digital audio recording system. Presented at 65th Audio Engineering Society Convention (London, 1980) preprint 1580(C1)

4

Error correction

The subject of error correction is almost always described in mathematical terms by specialists for the benefit of other specialists. Such mathematical approaches are quite inappropriate for a proper understanding of the concepts of error correction and only become necessary in order to analyse the quantitative behaviour of a system. The description given below will use the minimum possible amount of mathematics and it will then be seen that error correction is, in fact, quite straightforward.

4.1 Sensitivity of message to error

Before attempting to specify any piece of equipment it is necessary to quantify the problems to be overcome and to qualify how effectively they need to be overcome. For a digital recording or transmission system the causes of errors must be studied to quantify the problem, and the sensitivity of the destination to errors must be assessed. In computers there is tremendous sensitivity to errors in instructions. In audio and video the sensitivity to errors must be subjective. In both, the effect of a single bit in error depends upon the significance of the bit. If the least significant bit of a sample is wrong the chances are that the effect will be lost in the noise. Conversely, if a high order bit is in error a massive transient will be added to the sound or picture waveform. The effect of uncorrected errors in PCM audio sounds rather like vehicle ignition interference on a radio. The effect of errors in delta modulation is much smaller because every bit has the same significance and the information content of each bit is low.

If the error rate demanded by the destination cannot be met by the unaided channel, some form of error handling will be necessary. In some circumstances a delta-modulated system can be used with no error correction, but this is generally impossible in PCM.

4.2 Error mechanisms

Since digital data can be conveyed in many different ways, each having its own error mechanisms, it follows that there will be different approaches to protection of data. In addition, the kind of use to which a piece of equipment is put will make some error-protection schemes more practical than others.

Inside equipment, where data are conveyed in binary on wires, the noise resistance can be designed such that to all intents and purposes there will be no errors. For transmission between equipment there will be less control of the electromagnetic environment, and interference may corrupt binary data on wires, though not in optical fibres. Such interference will generally not correlate with the data. For long-distance transmission by wire there will be the effects of lightning and switching noise in exchanges to combat.

In MOS memories the datum is stored in a tiny charge-well which acts as a capacitor, and natural radioactive decay of the chip materials can cause alpha particles which have enough energy to discharge a well, resulting in a single-bit error. This only happens once every 30 years or so in a given chip, but when a great many chips are assembled to form a large memory for a computer the probability rises to one error every few minutes.

In magnetic recording there are many more mechanisms available to corrupt data, from mechanical problems such as media dropout and poor head contact, to Gaussian thermal noise in replay circuits and heads. In optical media the equivalent of dropout in manufacture is contamination of the optical layer by dust before it is sealed. In replay, surface contamination from fingerprints and birefringence in the transparent medium distort and diffuse the laser beam so that the reflected light pattern cannot be discerned.

Despite the difference in operating principle, magnetic recorders and optical media have similar effects when the corruption of data is studied. There are large isolated corruptions, called error bursts, where numerous bits are corrupted all together in an area which is otherwise error-free, and there are random errors affecting single bits or symbols. In the discussion of channel coding in Chapter 3 it was noted that wherever group codes are used a single corruption in a group renders all the data bits in that group meaningless. Thus single-bit errors are much less common in group-coded data.

Whatever the mechanism, the result will be that the received data will not be exactly the same as those sent. Sometimes it is enough to know that there has been an error, if time allows a retransmission to be arranged. This is quite feasible for telex messages but quite inappropriate for digital audio or video, which work in real time.

4.3 Error handling

Figure 4.1 shows the broad subdivisions of error handling. The first stage might well be called error avoidance and includes such measures as creating bad-block files in hard disks, placing digital audio blocks at the centre of the tape in D-1 format, and rewriting on a read-after-write error in computer tapes. Following these moves the data are entrusted to the channel, which causes whatever corruptions it feels like. On receipt of the data the occurrence of errors is first detected, and this process must be extremely reliable as it does not matter how fast the

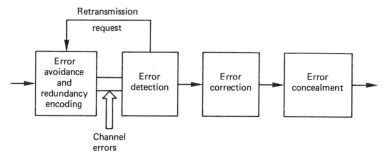

Figure 4.1 The major processes in an error-handling system

retry mechanism, how effective the correction, or how good the concealment algorithm if it is not known that they are necessary! The detection of an error then results in a course of action being decided. In a bidirectional link a retransmission could be requested. In a critical financial computer, reference to the backup file may be requested. In computer disk drives the detection of a read error frequently results in a retry. The disk is turning at typically 3600 rev/min and repeatedly presents the same data to a fixed head, making a retry very easy. Disk drives will also verify the data integrity of a new disk, and any blocks containing dropouts will be allocated to a hypothetical file which makes them appear to be already used. The computer will never write on them. Computer magnetic tape transports read the tape as it is being written and if an error is detected the transport will commonly reverse to the beginning of the block, erase a short length of tape, and try again. These are luxuries not available to digital audio or video recorders. The chore of verifying a tape before use would be unacceptable and in any case there is no guarantee that new tape defects will not arise in use. The non-contact rigid disk is much more consistent in this respect. It is reasonable to expect that the error handling of digital audio and video equipment will be more complex than that of computer equipment, especially when it is considered that some digital audio tape formats allow editing with a splicing block.

4.4 Interpolation

Although audio and video recorders are at a disadvantage with respect to computer recorders in that they cannot preformat and verify the medium, and there is no time for retries, they do have the advantage that there is a certain amount of redundancy in the information conveyed. If an error cannot be corrected, then it can be concealed. In audio systems, if a sample is lost it is possible to obtain an approximation to it by interpolating between adjacent values. Momentary interpolations in music are not serious but sustained use of interpolation restricts bandwidth and can cause aliasing if high frequencies are present. In advanced systems a spectral analysis of the sound is made and, if sample values are not available, samples having the same spectral characteristics are inserted. This concealment method is quite successful because the spectral shape changes relatively slowly in music. If there is too much corruption for concealment the only course is to mute.

In video recorders interpolation can be used in the same way as for audio, but there are additional possibilities, such as taking data from adjacent lines or from a previous field. Video concealment is a complex subject which will be dealt with in Chapter 5. In general, if use is to be made of concealment on replay, the data must generally be reordered or shuffled prior to recording. To take a simple example, odd-numbered samples are subject to a delay whereas even-numbered samples are undelayed. On playback this process must be reversed. If a gross error occurs on the tape following the reverse shuffle this will be broken into two separate error zones, one of which has corrupted odd samples, the other of which has corrupted even samples. Interpolation is then possible if the power of the correction system is exceeded.

4.5 Noise and probability

While it is generally stated that inside a piece of logic circuitry the binary signal is always greater than the noise, so that there will be no errors, the same is not true in high density recording. To see why this is so it is necessary to look at the characteristics of noise.

Noise is random and although under given conditions the noise power in a system may be constant, this value only determines the heat that would be developed in a resistive load. In digital recording, it is the instantaneous voltage of noise which is of interest since it is a form of interference which could alter the state of a binary signal if it were large enough. Unfortunately it cannot be predicted; indeed, if it could the interference could not be called noise. Noise can only be quantified statistically by measuring or predicting the likelihood of a given noise amplitude.

Figure 4.2 shows a graph relating the probability of occurrence to the amplitude of noise. The noise amplitude increases away from the origin along the horizontal axis and, for any amplitude of interest, the probability of that noise amplitude occurring can be read from the curve. The shape of the curve is

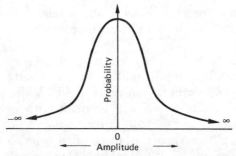

Figure 4.2 The probability of occurrence of noise of a given amplitude falls as that amplitude increases, but never reaches zero; as a consequence, however good signal-to-noise ratio may be, errors will still occur

known as a Gaussian distribution, which crops up whenever the overall effect of a large number of independent phenomena is considered. Magnetic recording depends on superimposing some average magnetism on vast numbers of magnetic particles.

If it were possible to isolate an individual noise generating microcosm of a tape or a head on the molecular scale, the noise it could generate would have physical limits due to the finite energy present. The noise distribution might then be rectangular, as shown in Figure 4.3(a), where all amplitudes below the physical limit are equally likely. If the combined effect of two of these microcosms is considered, clearly the maximum amplitude is now doubled because the two effects can add, but since the two effects are uncorrelated they can also subtract so the probability is no longer rectangular but becomes triangular, as shown in Figure 4.3(b). Probability falls to zero at peak amplitude because the chances of two independent mechanisms reaching their peak value with the same polarity at the same time are understandably small.

If the number of mechanisms summed together is now allowed to increase without limit the result is the Gaussian curve shown in Figure 4.3(c), where it will be seen that the curve has no limit because it is just possible that all mechanisms will simultaneously reach their peak value together, although the chances of this happening are incredibly remote.

Some conclusions can be drawn from the Gaussian distribution of noise.

Firstly, it is not possible to make error-free digital recordings because however high the signal to noise ratio of the recording

a)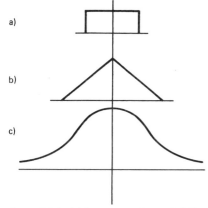

b)

c)

Figure 4.3 At (a) is a rectangular probability; all values are equally likely, but between physical limits. At (b) is the sum of two rectangular probabilities, which is triangular and at (c) is the Gaussian curve which is the sum of an infinite number of rectangular probabilities

there is still a small but finite chance that the noise can exceed the signal. Measuring the SNR of a channel establishes the noise power, which determines the width of the noise distribution curve relative to the signal amplitude. When in a binary system the noise amplitude exceeds the signal amplitude, a bit error will occur. Knowledge of the shape of the Gaussian curve allows the conversion of SNR into bit error rate (BER). It can be predicted how many bits will fail due to noise in a given recording but it is not possible to say which bits will be affected.

The logical reaction to this statement is to decide that error correction is necessary.

Error correction works by adding some bits to the data which are calculated from the data. This creates an entity called a codeword which spans a greater length of time than one bit alone. The statistics of noise mean that while one bit may be lost in a codeword, the loss of the rest of the codeword due to noise is highly improbable. As will be described later in this chapter, codewords are designed to be able to totally correct a finite number of corrupted bits. The greater the timespan over which the coding is performed, the greater will be the reliability achieved, although this does mean that an encoding delay will be experienced on recording, and a similar delay on reproduction. Shannon discovered that a message can be sent to any desired degree of accuracy provided that it is spread over a sufficient time span [1]. Engineers have to compromise because an infinite delay in the recovery of an error-free signal is not acceptable.

Having decided that error correction is necessary it is then only a small step to put it to maximum use. All error correction depends on adding bits to the original message and this of course increases the number of bits to be recorded, although it does not increase the information recorded. It might be imagined that error correction is going to reduce storage capacity because space has to be found for all the extra bits. Nothing could be further from the truth. Once an error correction system is used, the SNR of the channel can be reduced because the raised BER of the channel will be overcome by the error-correction system. Reduction of SNR by 3 dB in a magnetic tape track can be achieved by halving the track width, provided that the system is not dominated by head noise. This doubles the recording density, making the storage of the additional bits needed for error correction a trivial matter. In short, error correction is not a nuisance to be tolerated; it is a vital tool needed to maximize the efficiency of recorders. High density recording would not be possible without it.

Although the foregoing is true, error-correction systems must be able to handle burst errors due to dropouts as well as random errors due to noise.

4.6 Parity

The error-detection and correction processes are closely related and will be dealt with together here. The actual correction of an error is simplified tremendously by the adoption of binary. As there are only two symbols, zero and one, it is enough to know that a symbol is wrong, and the correct value is obvious. Figure 4.4 shows a minimal circuit required for correction once the bit in error has been identified. The exclusive–OR gate shows up extensively in error correction and the diagram also shows the truth table. One way of remembering the characteristics of this useful device is that there will be an output when the inputs are different. Inspection of the truth table will show that there is an even number of ones in each row (zero is an even number) and so the device could also be called an even-parity gate.

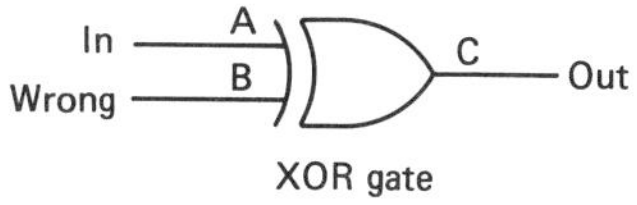

Truth table
of XOR gate

A	B	C
0	0	0
0	1	1
1	0	1
1	1	0

In ——— A

Wrong ——— B)) — C — Out

XOR gate

$A \oplus B = C$

Figure 4.4 Once the position of the error is identified, the correction process in binary is easy

Parity is a fundamental concept in error detection. In Figure 4.5, the example is given of a four-bit data word which is to be protected. If an extra bit is added to the word, which is calculated in such a way that the total number of ones in the five-bit word is even, this property can be tested on receipt. The generation of the parity bit in Figure 4.5 can be performed by a number of the ubiquitous XOR gates configured into what is known as a parity tree. In the diagram, if a bit is corrupted the received message will be seen to no longer have an even number of ones. If two bits are corrupted the failure will be undetected. This example can be used to introduce much of the terminology of error correction. The extra bit added to the message carries no information of its own since it is calculated from the other bits. It is therefore called a redundant bit. The addition of the redundant bit gives the message a special property, i.e. the number of ones is even. A message having some special property irrespective of the actual data content is called a codeword. All error correction relies on adding redundancy to real data to form codewords for transmission. If any corruption occurs the intention is that the received message will not have the special property; in other words if the received message is not a codeword there has definitely been an error. If the received message is a codeword there probably has not been an error. The word 'probably' must be used because the diagram shows that two bits in error will cause the received message to be a codeword, which cannot be discerned from an error-free message. If it is known that generally the only failure mechanism in the channel in question is loss of a single bit, it is *assumed* that receipt of a codeword means that there has been no error. If

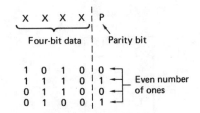

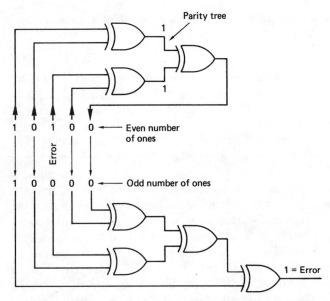

Figure 4.5 Parity checking adds up the number of ones in a word using, in this example, parity trees. One error bit and odd numbers of errors are detected. Even numbers of errors cannot be detected

there is a probability of two error bits, that becomes very nearly the probability of failing to detect an error since all odd numbers of errors will be detected and a four-bit error is much less likely. It is paramount in all error-correction systems that the protection used should be appropriate for the probability of errors to be encountered. An inadequate error-correction system is actually worse than not having any correction. Error correction works by trading probabilities. Error-free performance with a certain error rate is achieved at the expense of performance at higher error rates. Figure 4.6 shows the effect of

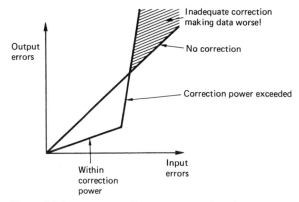

Figure 4.6 An error correction system can only reduce errors at normal error rates at the expense of increasing errors at higher rates. It is most important to keep a system working to the left of the knee in the graph

an error-correction system on the output error rate for a given raw, or input, error rate. It will be seen that there is a characteristic knee in the graph. If the expected raw error rate has been misjudged the consequences can be disastrous. Another result demonstrated by the example is that we can only guarantee to detect the same number of bits in error as there are redundant bits.

4.7 Wyner–Ash code

Despite its extreme simplicity, the principle of parity can be used to make an effective digital-audio error-correcting scheme. In the Wyner–Ash code employed in some early BBC work [2], four tape tracks were required to convey one digital audio channel, which reduced the linear speed of the tape and reduced the impact of a dropout on the data. Figure 4.7(a) shows that alternate tracks carried data and parity bits computed from running pairs of data bits. With this mechanism data-track errors always cause an even number of parity failures, and Figure 4.7(b) shows an example of how such an error can be corrected. Parity-track errors, however, cause single-parity failures, which can be neglected, as shown in Figure 4.7(c). While this technique is successful it requires an overhead of

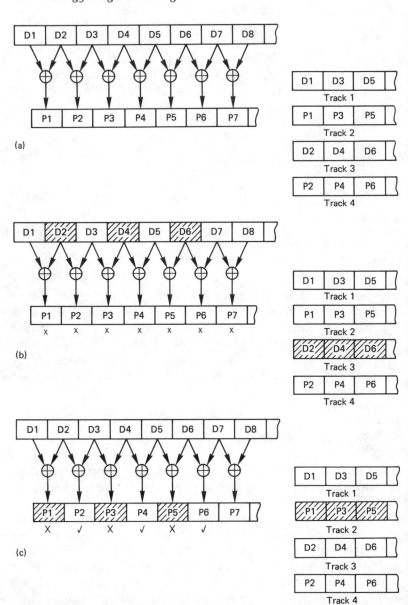

Figure 4.7 In the Wyner–Ash coding illustrated here, there is 100% overhead due to the additional parity symbols. The data and parity are distributed over the tape tracks, as shown in (a). At (b) a burst error in a data track causes continuous parity errors as shown, and correction can be performed. For example, D2 = D1 ⊕ P1, etc. At (c) a burst error in a parity track causes alternate parity errors which can be ignored

100% redundancy, which implies that tape consumption must suffer. Codes which need less overhead are inevitably more complex, however.

4.8 Crossword code

In the example of Figure 4.5 the error was detected but it was not possible to say which bit was in error. Even though the code used can only detect errors, correction is still possible if a suitable strategy is used. Figure 4.8 shows the use of a crossword code, also known as a product code. The data are formed into a two-dimensional array, with parity taken on rows and columns.

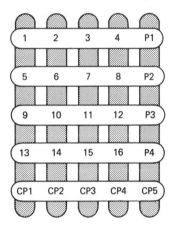

Figure 4.8 A crossword parity-check system. Horizontal checks are made by P1, P2, and cross parity checks on columns are made by CP1, CP2, etc. If, for example, bit 10 were in error, it would be located by CP2 and P3 intersecting

If a single bit fails, one row check and one column check will fail and the failing bit can be located at the intersection of the two failing checks. Although two bits in error confuse this simple scheme, using more complex coding in a two-dimensional structure is very powerful and further examples will be given throughout this chapter.

4.9 Hamming code

In a one-dimensional code the position of the failing bit can be determined by using more parity checks. In Figure 4.9 the four data bits have been used to compute three redundancy bits, making a seven-bit codeword. The four data bits are examined in turn, and each bit which is a one will cause the corresponding

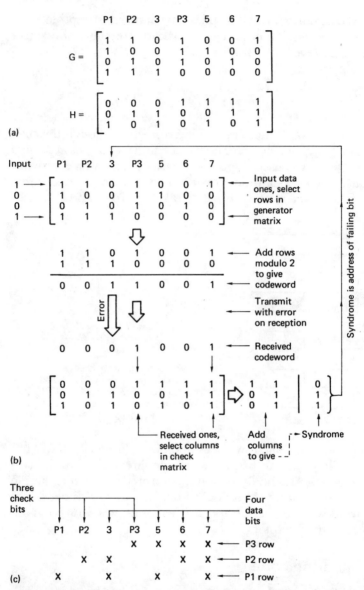

Figure 4.9 (a) The generator and check matrices of a Hamming code. The data and check bits are arranged as shown because it causes the syndrome to be the binary address of the failing bit. (b) An example of Hamming-code generation and error correction. (c) Another way of looking at Hamming code is to say that the rows of crosses in this chart are calculated to have even parity. If bit 3 fails, parity check P3 is not affected, but parity checks P1 and P2 both include bit 3 and will fail

row of a generator matrix to be added to an exclusive–OR sum. For example, if the data were 1001, the top and bottom rows of the matrix would be XORed. The matrix used is known as an identity matrix because the data bits in the codeword are identical to the data bits to be conveyed. This is useful because the original data can be stored unmodified and the check bits are simply attached to the end to make a so-called systematic codeword. Almost all digital recording equipment uses systematic codes. The way in which the redundancy bits are calculated is simply that they do not all use every data bit. If a data bit has not been included in a parity check it can fail without affecting the outcome of that check. The position of the error is deduced from the pattern of successful and unsuccessful checks in the check matrix. This pattern is known as a syndrome.

The example of a failing bit is given in the diagram. Bit three fails, and because this bit is included in only two of the checks, there are two ones in the failure pattern, 011. As some care was taken in designing the matrix pattern for the generation of the check bits the syndrome, 011, is the address of the failing bit. This is the fundamental feature of the Hamming codes due to Richard Hamming [3]. The performance of this seven-bit code word can be assessed. In seven bits there can be 128 combinations, but in four data bits there are only 16 combinations. Thus out of 128 possible received messages only 16 will be codewords, so if the message is completely trashed by a gross corruption it will still be possible to detect that this has happened 112 times out of 127 because in these cases the syndrome will be non-zero (the 128th case is the correct data). There is thus only a probability of detecting that the whole of the message is corrupt. In an idle moment it is possible to work out, in a similar way, the number of false codewords which can result from different numbers of bits being assumed to have failed. For less than three bits the failure will always be detected because there are three check bits. Returning to the example, if two bits fail there will be a non-zero syndrome, but if this is used to point to a bit in error a miscorrection will result. From these results can be deduced another important feature of error codes. The power of detection is always greater than the power of correction, which is also fortunate since if the correcting power is exceeded by an error it will at least be a known problem and steps can taken to prevent any undesirable consequences.

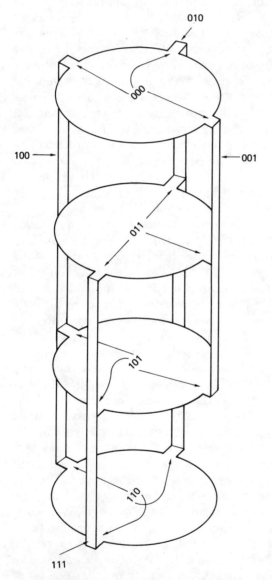

Figure 4.10 Hamming distance of 2. The disk centres contain codewords. Corrupting each bit in turn produces the distance 1 values on the vertical members. In order to change one codeword to another, two bits must be changed so the code has a Hamming distance of 2

4.10 Hamming distance

It is useful at this point to introduce the concept of Hamming distance. This is the minimum number of bits that must be changed in any codeword without turning it into another codeword. Clearly, if errors corrupt a codeword so that it is no longer a codeword it will definitely be detectable and possibly correctable. If errors convert one codeword into another it will not even be detected.

Figure 4.10 shows Hamming distance diagrammatically. A three-bit codeword is used with two data bits and one parity bit. With three bits a received code could have eight combinations, but only four of these will be codewords. The valid codewords are shown in the centre of each of the disks and these will be seen to be identical to the rows of the truth table in Figure 4.4. At the perimeter of the disks are shown the received words which would result from a single-bit error, i.e. they have a Hamming distance of 1. It will be seen that the same received word (on the vertical bars) can be obtained from a different single-bit corruption of any three codewords. It is thus not possible to tell which codeword was corrupted and so, although all single-bit errors can be detected, correction is not possible. This diagram should be compared with that of Figure 4.11, which is a Venn diagram

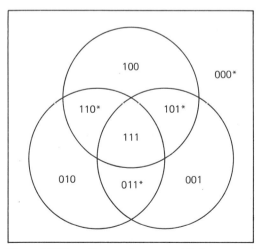

Figure 4.11 Venn diagram shows a one bit change crossing any boundary which is a Hamming distance of one. Compare with Figure 4.10. Codewords marked*

where there is a set in which the MSB is 1 (upper circle), a set in which the middle bit is 1 (lower left circle), and a set in which the LSB is 1 (lower right circle). Note that in crossing any boundary only one bit changes and so each boundary represents a Hamming distance change of 1. The four codewords of Figure 4.10 are repeated here and it will be seen that single-bit errors in any codeword produces a non-codeword and so single-bit errors are always detectable.

Correction is possible if the number of non-codewords is increased by increasing the number of redundant bits. This means that it is possible to spread out the actual codewords in Hamming distance terms.

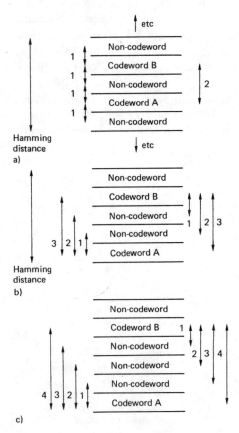

Figure 4.12 (a) Distance 2 code, non-codewords are at distance 1 from *two* possible codewords so it cannot be deduced what the current one is. (b) Distance 3 code, non-codewords which have *single-bit errors* can be attributed to the nearest codeword. Breaks down in presence of double-bit errors. (c) Distance 4 code, non-codewords which have single-bit errors can be attributed to the nearest codeword, AND double bit errors form *different* non-codewords, and can thus be detected but not corrected

Figure 4.12(a) shows a distance 2 code, where there is only one redundancy bit, and so half of the possible words will be codewords. There will be non-codewords at distance 1 which can be produced by altering a single bit in either of two codewords. In this case it is not possible to tell what the original codeword was in the case of a single-bit error.

Figure 4.12(b) shows a distance 3 code, where there will now be at least two non-codewords between codewords. If a single-bit error occurs in a code word, the resulting non-codeword will be at distance 1 from the original codeword. This same non-codeword could also have been produced by changing *two* bits in a different codeword. If it is known that the failure mechanism is a single bit it can be *assumed* that the original codeword was the one closest in Hamming distance to the received bit pattern, and so correction is possible. If, however, our assumption about the error mechanism proved to be wrong and in fact a two-bit error had occurred, this assumption would take us to the wrong codeword, turning the event into a three-bit error. This is an illustration of the knee in the graph of Figure 4.6, where if the power of the code is exceeded it makes things worse.

Figure 4.12(c) shows a distance 4 code. There are now three non-codewords between codewords and, clearly, single-bit errors can still be corrected by choosing the nearest codeword. Double-bit errors will be detected because they result in non-codewords equidistant in Hamming terms from codewords, but it is not possible to say what the original codeword was.

Figure 4.13 shows a more complex arrangement of the 16 possible combinations of four bits. Travelling along any of the ties between disks is the equivalent of a Hamming distance of 1. The equivalent Venn diagram is shown in Figure 4.14. At this point the Venn diagram no longer shows the whole story because, although there is still a Hamming distance of 1 when crossing a boundary, some of the areas have only three sides so not all possible changes are shown and it is necessary to add a magic tunnel whose length is a Hamming distance of 1, to allow all single-bit changes to be followed.

Unfortunately, attempts to draw more complex Hamming distance diagrams for longer wordlengths result in a real mess because the number of tunnels needed rises sharply. It is, however, possible to draw Venn diagrams to almost any number of bits [4], which will show Hamming distance in a restricted

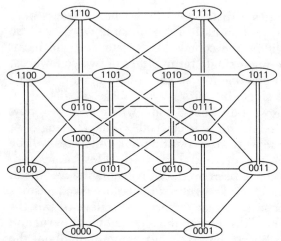

Figure 4.13 Hamming distance diagram for four bits. Each bond between the disks is unit Hamming distance

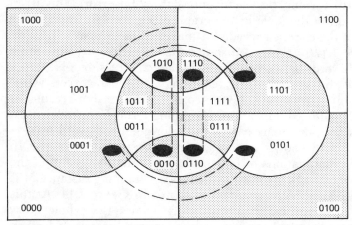

Figure 4.14 Modified Venn diagram which also shows Hamming distance. A Hamming distance of one can be obtained by crossing any one boundary, or by travelling down a magic tunnel

sense. Inside the back cover of this book is a seven-bit Venn diagram, which needs to be made into a cylinder using a couple of paper clips. The cylindrical diagram results from mapping a diagram which was originally spherical so the bands at top and bottom are essentially the poles, and the line across the middle is the equator. There are 128 different combinations of seven bits and these change one bit at a time when moving across a logical boundary. Following the sequence of numbers along the equator in fact results in a Gray code. As we are attempting to draw a multidimensional vector space on a flat piece of paper only some of the dimensions will work. The polar areas 0000000 and 1111111 work because each has seven boundaries and all seven possible single-bit changes can be followed. The two largest islands 0100000 and 1011111 also show this feature because they also have seven logical sides. On the diagram, all 16 codewords of the Hamming code of Section 4.9 have been marked with a dot. Note that 0000000 and 0100000 are both codewords and they display the minimum Hamming distance of 3, since it is necessary to cross over three boundaries to get from one to the other. In the case of an error, 0100000 might be received and this can be found adjacent to 0000000. As the received word is not a codeword the error has been detected. Now 0100000 could have resulted from a single-bit corruption of 0000000, or from a two-bit corruption of the codeword 0100011, a Hamming distance of 2 away. If it is assumed correctly that only single-bit errors occur, the nearest codeword in Hamming distance terms will be chosen to find the correct message, namely 0000000. However, if the assumption was wrong and a two-bit error did in fact occur, then the original message would have been 0100011, which will be miscorrected to 0000000. In other words a two-bit error is made into a three-bit error by the miscorrection. Clearly, a distance 3 system can only be used to correct single-bit errors at the expense of introducing three-bit errors occasionally, as was illustrated by the knee in the graph of Figure 4.6.

4.11 Applications of Hamming code

The Hamming codes are used in computer memories where the failure mechanism is that of single bits. The efficiency in terms of storage needed is not very good in the simple example of Figure 4.9, as three check bits are needed for only four data bits. Since the failing bit is determined using a binary split mechanism, it follows that doubling the amount of data will only require one extra check bit, provided that the number of errors to be detected remains the same. Thus for the smallest proportion of redundancy, long codewords should be used. In computer memories these codewords are typically four or eight data bytes in length, plus redundancy. A drawback of long codewords for computer memory applications is that if it is required to change only one byte in the memory the whole word has to be read, corrected, modified, encoded and stored again – a so-called read–modify–write cycle. The codes for computer memories will generally have an extra check bit which allows the occurrence of a double-bit error always to be detected but not corrected. If this happens the syndrome will be the address of a bit which is outside the data word. Such codes are known as SECDED (single error-correcting double error-detecting) codes. The Hamming distance of these codes is one greater than the equivalent SEC (single-error correcting) code.

The correction of one bit is of little use in the presence of burst errors, but a Hamming code can be made to correct burst errors by using interleaving. Figure 4.15 shows that if several codewords are calculated beforehand, and woven together as shown before they are sent down the channel, then a burst of errors which corrupts several bits will become a number of single-bit errors in separate codewords upon deinterleaving. Interleaving is used extensively in digital recording and will be discussed in greater detail later in this chapter.

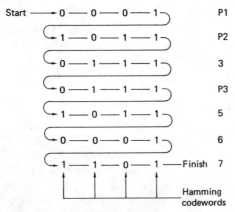

Figure 4.15 The vertical columns of this diagram are all codewords generated by the matrix of Figure **4.9** which can correct a single-bit error. If these words are recorded in the order shown, a burst error of up to four bits will result in one single-bit error in each codeword, which is correctable. Interleave requires memory, and causes delay. Deinterleave requires the same

4.12 Cyclic codes

The implementation of a Hamming code can very quickly be carried out using parity trees, which is ideal for memory applications where access time is increased by the correction process. However, in most audio applications the data are stored serially, such as on a magnetic or optical track, and it is desirable to use relatively large data blocks to reduce the amount of the medium devoted to preambles, addressing and synchronizing. Where large data blocks are to be handled the use of a lookup table or tree has to be abandoned because it would become impossibly large. The principle of generator and check matrices will still be employed but they will be matrices which can be generated algorithmically by an equation. The syndrome will then be converted to the bit(s) in error, not by looking them up, but by solving an equation.

Where data can be accessed serially, simpler circuitry can be used because the same gate will be used for many XOR operations. Unfortunately the reduction in component count is only paralleled by an increase in the difficulty of explaining what takes place.

The circuit of Figure 4.16 is a kind of shift register, but with a peculiar feedback arrangement which leads it to be known as a twisted-ring counter. If seven message bits A–G are applied serially to this circuit and each one of them is clocked, the outcome can be followed in the diagram. As bit A is presented and the system is clocked, bit A will enter the left-hand latch. When bits B and C are presented A moves across to the right. Both XOR gates will have A on the upper input from the right-hand latch; the left one has D on the lower input and the right one has B on the lower input. When clocked the left latch will thus be loaded with the XOR of A and D, and the right one with the XOR of A and B. The remainder of the sequence can be followed, bearing in mind that when the same term appears on both inputs of an XOR gate it goes out as the exclusive OR of something, with itself is nothing. At the end of the process the latches contain three different expressions. Essentially, the circuit makes three parity checks through the message, leaving the result of each in the three stages of the register. In the diagram these expressions have been used to draw up a check matrix. The significance of these steps can now be explained.

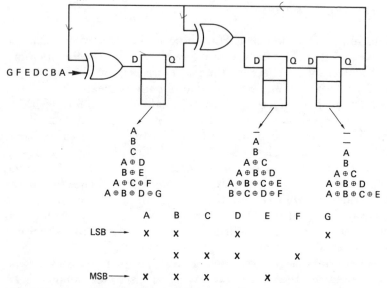

Figure 4.16 When seven successive bits A–G are clocked into this circuit, the contents of the three latches are shown for each clock. The final result is a parity-check matrix

The bits A B C and D are four data bits, and the bits E F and G are redundancy. When the redundancy is calculated, bit E is chosen so that there are an even number of ones in bits A B C and E; bit F is chosen such that the same applies to bits B C D and F; and similarly for bit G. Thus the four data bits and the three check bits form a seven-bit codeword. If there is no error in the codeword when it is fed into the circuit shown, the result of each of the three parity checks will be zero and every stage of the shift register will be cleared. If a bit in the codeword is corrupted there will be a non-zero result. For example, if bit D fails, the check on bits A B D and G will fail and a one will appear in the left-hand latch. The check on bits B C D F will also fail and the centre latch will set. The check on bits A B C E will not fail because D is not involved in it, making the right-hand bit zero. There will be a syndrome of 110 in the register and this will be seen from the check matrix to correspond to an error in bit D. Whichever bit fails there will be a different three-bit syndrome which uniquely identifies the failed bit. As there are only three latches, there can be eight different syndromes. One of these is zero, which is the error-free condition, and so there are seven remaining error syndromes. The length of the codeword cannot exceed seven bits or there would not be enough syndromes to correct all of the bits. This can also be made to tie in with the generation of the check matrix. If 14 bits, A–N, were fed into the circuit shown, the result would be that the check matrix repeated twice, and if a syndrome of 101 were to result it could not be determined whether bit D or bit K failed. Because the check repeats every seven bits the code is said to be a cyclic redundancy check (CRC) code.

In Figure 4.9 an example of a Hamming code was given. Comparison of the check matrix of Figure 4.16 with that of Figure 4.9 will show that the only difference is the order of the matrix columns. The two different processes have thus achieved exactly the same results and the performance of both must be identical. This is not true in general, but these examples have been selected to allow parallels to be seen. In practice, Hamming code blocks will generally be much smaller than the blocks used in CRC codes.

It has been seen that the circuit shown makes a matrix check on a received word to determine if there has been an error, but the same circuit can also be used to generate the check bits. To visualize how this is done examine what happens if only the data bits A B C and D are known and the check bits E F and G are set to zero. If this message, ABCD000, is fed into the circuit the left-hand latch will then contain the XOR of A B C and zero, which is of course what E should be. The centre latch will contain the XOR of B C D and zero, which is what F should be, and so on. This process is not quite ideal, however, because it is necessary to wait for three clock periods after entering the data before the check bits are available. Where the data are simultaneously being recorded and fed into the encoder the delay would prevent the check bits being easily added to the end of the data stream. This problem can be overcome by slightly modifying the encoder circuit, as shown in Figure 4.17. By moving the position of the input to the right, the operation of the circuit is advanced so that the check bits are ready after only four clocks. The process can be followed in the diagram for the four data bits A B C and D. On the first clock bit A enters the left two latches, whereas on the second clock bit B will appear on the upper input of the left XOR gate, with bit A on the lower input, causing the centre latch to load the XOR of A and B, and so on.

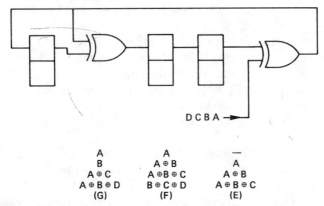

A	A	—
B	A ⊕ B	A
A ⊕ C	A ⊕ B ⊕ C	A ⊕ B
A ⊕ B ⊕ D	B ⊕ C ⊕ D	A ⊕ B ⊕ C
(G)	(F)	(E)

Figure 4.17 By moving the insertion point three places to the right, the calculation of the check bits is completed in only four clock periods and they can follow the data immediately. This is equivalent to premultiplying the data by x^3

The way in which the correction system works has been described in engineering terms but it can be described mathematically if analysis is contemplated.

Just as the position of a decimal digit in a number determines the power of 10 (whether that digit means 1, 10 or a 100), the position of a binary digit determines the power of 2 (whether it means 1, 2 or 4). It is possible to rewrite a binary number so that it is expressed as a list of powers of 2. For example, the binary number 1101 means $8 + 4 + 1$, and can be written

$$2^3 + 2^2 + 2^0$$

In fact, much of the theory of error correction applies to symbols in number bases other than 2, so that the number can also be written more generally as

$$x^3 + x^2 + 1 \ (2^0 = 1)$$

which also looks much more impressive. This expression, containing as it does various powers, is of course a polynomial, and the circuit of Figure 4.16, which has been seen to construct a parity-check matrix on a codeword, can also be described as calculating the remainder due to dividing the input by a polynomial using modulo-2 arithmetic. In modulo-2 there are no borrows or carries, and addition and subtraction are replaced by the XOR function, which makes hardware implementation very easy. In Figure 4.18 it will be seen that the circuit of Figure 4.16 actually divides the codeword by a polynomial which is

$$x^3 + x + 1 \text{ or } 1011$$

This can be deduced from the fact that the right-hand bit is fed into several lower order stages of the register at once. Once all

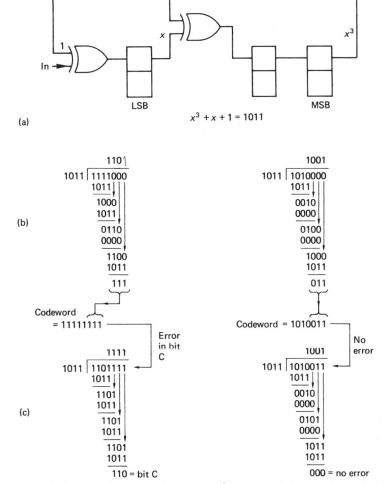

Figure 4.18 Circuit of Figure **4.16** divided by $x^3 + x + 1$ to find remainder. At (b) this is used to calculate check bits. At (c) left, there is an error, non-zero syndrome 110 points to bit C. At (c) right, zero syndrome, no error

the bits of the message have been clocked in, the circuit contains the remainder. In mathematical terms the special property of a codeword is that it is a polynomial which yields a remainder of zero when divided by the generating polynomial. If an error has occurred it is considered that this is due to an error polynomial which has been added to the codeword polynomial. If a codeword divided by the check polynomial is zero, a non-zero syndrome must represent the error polynomial divided by the check polynomial. Some examples of modulo-2 division are given in Figure 4.18 which can be compared with the parallel computation of parity checks according to the matrix of Figure 4.16.

The process of generating the codeword from the original data can also be described mathematically. If a codeword has to give zero remainder when divided, it follows that the data can be converted to a codeword by adding the remainder when the data is divided. Generally speaking, the remainder would have to be subtracted, but in modulo-2 there is no distinction. This process is also illustrated in Figure 4.18. The four data bits have three zeros placed on the right-hand end to make the wordlength equal to that of a codeword, and this word is then divided by the polynomial to calculate the remainder. The remainder is added to the zero-extended data to form a codeword. The modified circuit of Figure 4.17 can be described as premultiplying the data by x^3 before dividing.

It is also interesting to study the operation of the circuit of Figure 4.16 with no input. Whatever the starting condition of the three bits in the latches the same state will always be reached again after seven clocks, except if zero is used. The states of the latches form an endless ring of non-sequential numbers called a Galois field, after the French mathematical prodigy Evariste Galois who discovered them. The states of the circuit form a maximum-length sequence because there are as many states as are permitted by the wordlength. As the all-zeros case is disallowed, the maximum length sequence generated by a register of m bits cannot exceed $(2^m - 1)$ states, which will also be the length of the codeword in simple cyclic codes. The Galois field, however, includes the zero term. It is interesting to explore the bizarre mathematics of Galois fields which use modulo-2 arithmetic (exclusively!). Familiarity with such manipulations is useful when studying more advanced codes.

As the circuit of Figure 4.16 divides the input by the function $F(x) = x^3 + x + 1$, and there is no input in this case, the operation of the circuit has to be described by

$$x^3 + x + 1 = 0$$

Each three-bit state of the circuit can be described by combinations of powers of x, such as

$$x^2 = 100$$

$$x = 010$$

$$x^2 + x = 110, \text{ etc.}$$

To avoid confusion, the three-bit state of the field will be called a, which is a primitive element. Now,

$$a^3 + a + 1 = 0$$

In modulo 2,

$$a + a = a^2 + a^2 = 0$$

$$a = x = 010$$

$$a^2 = x^2 = 100$$

$$a^3 = a + 1 = 011$$

$$a^4 = a \times a^3 = a(a + 1) = a^2 + a = 110$$

$$a^5 = a^2 + a + 1 = 111$$

$$a^6 = a \times a^5 = a(a^2 + a + 1)$$

$$= a^3 + a^2 + a = a + 1 + a^2 + a$$

$$= a^2 + 1 = 101$$

$$a^7 = a(a^2 + 1) = a^3 + a$$

$$= a + 1 + a = 1 = 001$$

In this way it can be seen that the complete set of elements of the Galois field can be expressed by successive powers of the primitive element. Note that the twisted-ring circuit of Figure 4.16 simply raises a to higher and higher powers as it is clocked; thus the seemingly complex multibit changes caused by a single clock of the register become simple to calculate using the correct primitive and the appropriate power.

Cyclic redundancy codes are of primary importance for detecting errors and several have been standardized for use in digital communications. The most common of these are

$$x^{16} + x^{15} + x^2 + 1 \text{ (CRC–16)}$$

$$x^{16} + x^{12} + x^5 + 1 \text{ (CRC–CCITT)}$$

Integrated circuits are available which contain all the necessary circuitry to generate and check redundancy [5]. A representative chip is the Fairchild 9401 which will be found in a great deal of equipment because it implements the above polynomials in addition to some others. A feature of the chip is that the feedback register can be configured to work backwards if required. The required polynomial is selected by a three-bit control code, as shown in Figure 4.19. The desired code is implemented by enabling different feedback connections to be kept in a ROM. The data stream to be recorded is clocked in serially, with the control signal CWE (check word enable) true.

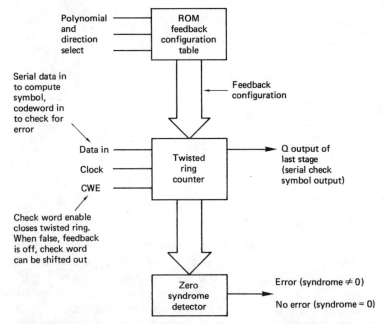

Figure 4.19 Simplified block by CRC chip which can implement several polynomials, and both generate and check redundancy

At the end of the data this signal is made false and turns off the feedback so that the device behaves as an ordinary shift register and the check bits can be clocked out of the Q output and appended to the recording. Upon playback the entire codeword is clocked into the device with CWE true and at the end of the codeword, if the register contains all zeros, the error output will be false, whereas if the syndrome is non-zero it will be true.

The output of such a chip is binary; either there was an error or (with high probability) there was not. There is no indication where the error was. Nevertheless, an effective error-correction system can be made using a product or crossword code. An example of this is the error-correction system of the Sony PCM-1610/1630 unit used for Compact Disc mastering. Figure 4.20 shows that in this system two sets of three audio samples have a cyclic redundancy check character (CRCC) added to form codewords. Three parity words are generated by taking the exclusive–OR of the two sets of samples, and a CRCC is added to this also. If an error occurs in one sample the CRC for the codeword containing that sample will fail and *all* samples in the codeword will be deemed to be in error. The sample can be corrected by taking the exclusive–OR of the other samples and the parity words. The error detector simply serves as a pointer to a separate correction mechanism. This technique is often

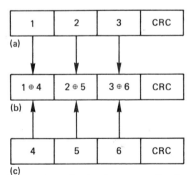

(a)

(b)

(c)

Figure 4.20 The simple crossword code of the PCM 1610/1630 format. Horizontal codewords are cyclic polynomials; vertical codewords are simple parity. Cyclic code detects errors and acts as erasure pointer for parity correction. For example, if word 2 fails, CRC (a) fails, and 1, 2, and 3 are all erased. The correct values are computed from (b) and (c) such that:

$1 = (1 \oplus 4) \oplus 4$
$2 - (2 \oplus 5) \oplus 5$
$3 = (3 \oplus 6) \oplus 6$

referred to as correction by erasure. The error detector erases the samples which are in error so that the corrector knows which ones to correct. If the error is in the parity words no action need be taken. It will be seen that there is 100% redundancy in this simple format, but the unit is intended to operate with a standard video recorder whose bandwidth is predefined, thus there would be no saving involved in using a code with less overhead.

4.13 Burst correction

The concept of Hamming distance has been introduced in the context of single-bit correction. However, it can be extended to explain how more than one bit can be corrected. In Figure 4.21 the example of two bits in error is given. If a codeword four bits long suffers a single-bit error it could produce one of four different words. If it suffers a two-bit error it could produce one of $3 + 2 + 1$ different words, as shown in the diagram (the error bits are underlined). The total number of possible words of Hamming distance 1 or 2 from a four-bit codeword is thus

$$4 + 3 + 2 + 1 = 10$$

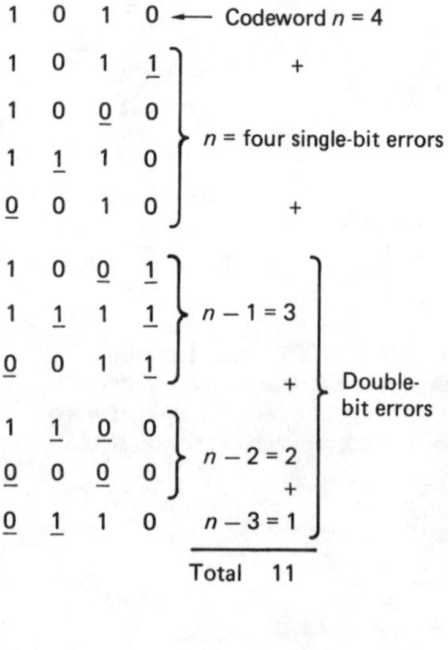

Figure 4.21 Where double-bit errors occur, the number of patterns necessary is $(n - 1) + (n - 2) + (n - 3) + \dots$ etc. Total necessary is $1 + n + (n - 1) + (n - 2) + (n - 3) + \dots$ etc. Example here is of four bits, and all possible patterns up to Hamming distance of 2 are shown (errors underlined)

If the two-bit error is to be correctable, no other codeword can be allowed to become one of this number of error patterns due to a two-bit error of its own. Thus every codeword requires space for itself plus all possible error patterns of Hamming distance 2 or 1, which is 11 patterns in this example. Clearly, there are only 16 patterns available in a four-bit code, and thus no data can be conveyed if two-bit protection is necessary.

The number of different patterns possible in a word of n bits is

$$1 + n + (n - 1) + (n - 2) + (n - 3) + \ldots$$

and this pattern range has to be shared between the ranges of each codeword without overlap. For example, an eight-bit codeword could result in $1 + 8 + 7 + 6 + 5 + 4 + 3 + 2 + 1 = 37$ patterns. As there are only 256 patterns in eight bits, it follows that only 256/37/7 pieces of information can be conveyed. The nearest integer below is 6, and the nearest power of 2 below is 4, which corresponds to two data bits and six check bits in the eight-bit word. The amount of redundancy necessary to correct *any* two bits in error is large and, as the number of bits to be corrected grows, the redundancy necessary becomes enormous and impracticable. A further problem is that the more redundancy is added the greater the probability of an error in a codeword. Fortunately, in practice, errors occur in bursts as has already been described, and it is a happy consequence that the number of patterns that result from the corruption of a codeword by *adjacent* two-bit errors is much smaller.

It can be deduced that the number of redundant bits necessary to correct a burst error is twice the number of bits in the burst for a perfect code. This is done by working out the number of received messages which could result from corruption of the codeword by bursts of from one bit up to the largest burst size allowed and then making sure that there are enough redundant bits to allow that number of combinations in the received message.

Some codes, such as the Fire code due to Philip Fire [6], are designed to correct single bursts in the codeword, whereas later codes, such as the B-adjacent code due to Bossen, could correct two bursts [7]. The Reed–Solomon codes (Irving Reed and Gustave Solomon [8]) have the extremely useful feature that the number of bursts which are correctable can be chosen at the design stage by the amount of redundancy.

4.14 Fire code

The operation of a Fire code will now be illustrated. A data block has deliberately been made small for the purposes of illustration in Figure 4.22(a). The matrix for generating parity bits on the data is shown beneath the block. In each horizontal row of the matrix, the presence of an X means that the data bit in that column has been counted in a parity check. The five rows result in five parity bits which are appended to the data. The simple circuit needed to generate this check word is also shown. The same codeword corrupted by three errors is shown in Figure 4.22(b). The matrix check now results in a different check code. An exclusive–OR between the original and the new check words gives the error syndrome. Figure 4.22(c) shows a different error condition which results in the same syndrome, an ambiguity which must be resolved. The method of doing this, which is fundamental to Fire code, follows. The definition of a burst of length b bits is that the first and last bits must be wrong, but the intervening $b - 2$ bits may or may not be wrong. As the presence of a one in a syndrome shows there is a bit in error, another way of stating this is that a burst syndrome of length b cannot contain

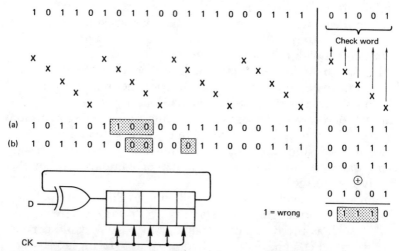

Figure 4.22 This matrix develops a burst-detecting code with circuit shown. On reading, the same encoding process is used, and the two checkwords are XOR-gated. Two examples of error bursts shown (a, b) give the same syndrome; this ambiguity is resolved by the technique of Figure **4.23**

more than $b - 2$ zeros between the ones. If the number of check bits used to correct a burst of length b is increased to $2b - 1$, then a burst of length b can be unambiguously defined by shifting the syndrome and looking for $b - 1$ successive zeros. Since the burst cannot contain more than $b - 2$ zeros, the $b - 1$ zeros must lie outside the burst. Figure 4.23 gives an example of the process and shows that the number of shifts necessary to put the $b - 1$ zeros at the left-hand side of the register is equal to the distance of the burst edge from the previous $n \times (2b - 1)$th bit boundary. The b right-hand bits will be the burst pattern, and if the received bits are inverted wherever a one appears in this pattern, correction will be achieved. Obviously if the burst exceeds b bits long, the $b - 1$ contiguous zeros will never be found and correction is impossible. Using this approach alone it is not possible to determine what the value of n is. The burst has been defined but its location is not known. To locate the burst requires the use of a cyclic polynomial code described earlier. A burst-correcting Fire code is made by combining the expression for the burst-defining code with the expression for the burst-locating polynomial. If the burst-locating polynomial appends an m bit remainder to the data, the check word will consist of $m + 2b - 1$ bits, and the codeword length n becomes

$$n = (2^m - 1) \times (2b - 1) \text{ bits}$$

Figure 4.24 shows the synthesis of a Fire code from the two parts, with the polynomial expressions for comparison with the necessary hardware. During writing, k serial data bits are shifted into the circuit, and $n - k$ check bits are shifted out to give a codeword of length n. On reading, the codeword is shifted into the same circuit and should result in an all-zero syndrome if there has been no error, as shown in Figure 4.25. If there is a non-zero syndrome there has been an error. As all data blocks are recorded as codewords the effect of the actual data on the check circuit is to give a zero remainder. The only effect on the syndrome is due to the errors. Any non-zero syndrome represents the exclusive–OR function of what the data should have been and what it was. This function has, however, been shifted an unknown number of times. The error burst is one state of a Galois field and the error burst is another. Any state of the Galois field can be reached from any other by shifting, so if the syndrome is shifted, sooner or later the error burst will show up.

114

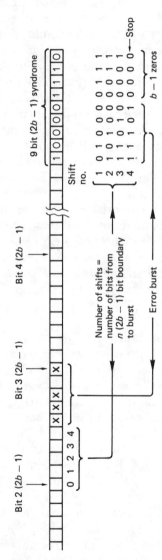

Figure 4.23 Burst of length b bits can only contain $b - 2$ zeros, so $b - 1$ zeros cannot be in a burst. By shifting the syndrome until $b - 1$ zeros are detected, the burst is defined unambiguously. The number of shifts needed gives the positon of the burst relative to the previous $n(2b - 1)$th bit boundary. In this example $b = 5$, hence $2b - 1 = 9$ and the boundaries referred to will be at bits 9, 18, 27, etc. A burst of up to nine bits can be detected but not corrected. Only the nature of the burst is defined by this process; its position has to be determined independently

115

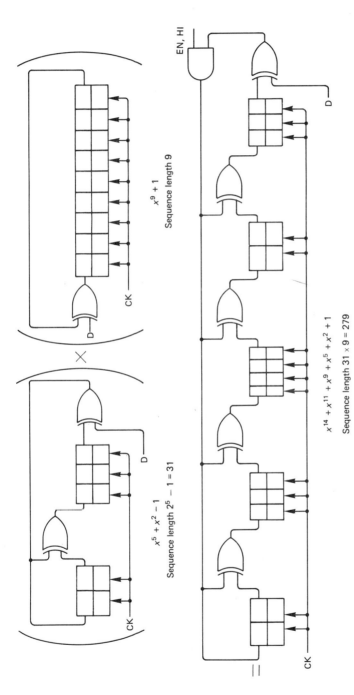

Figure 4.24 Derivation of Fire code from two fundamental expressions, together with encoding circuits. From the codeword length of 279 bits, 14 are check bits, making this a (279: 265) code

116

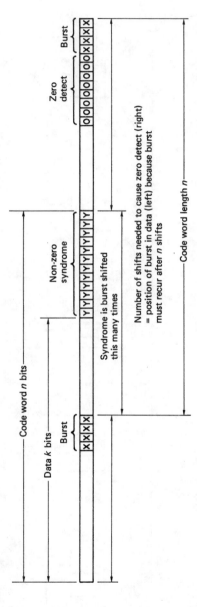

Figure 4.25 Owing to the characteristics of Galois fields, syndrome Y is simply the error burst which has been shifted a number of times equal to the number of bits from the burst to the end of the code word. As the field repeats every *n* shifts, it is only necessary to shift the syndrome and count the number of shifts necessary to give a zero detect condition. This number is equal to the position of the burst in the data. If no zero condition is found, then the burst is longer than *b* and cannot be corrected. It is, however, important to detect uncorrectable errors. The example can detect all bursts up to the length of the check word *n* − *k*; beyond this a statistical element is introduced

The only remaining question is how it will be recognized. The only ones in the correct state of the Galois field will be those representing the burst and they will be confined to the last b stages of the register. All other stages of the register will be zero. Owing to the highly non-sequential nature of Galois fields there is no possibility of $n - k - b$ contiguous zeros being found in any other state. The number of shifts required to arrive at this condition must be counted because it is equal to the distance from the beginning of the block to the burst. In most Fire-code applications the parameter b will be chosen to exceed the typical burst size of the channel and m to achieve the desired probability of undetected error. This usually results in a codeword of enormous size, much longer than the data blocks used on most disk drives. For example, the Fire code used in many IBM disk drives uses the polynomial

$$(x^{21} + 1) \ (x^{11} + x^2 + 1)$$

which gives a codeword of length

$$(2^{11} - 1) \times 21 = 42\,987 \text{ bits } (42\,955 \text{ data bits})$$

In practice this is not a problem. The data block can be made shorter than the codeword by a technique known as puncturing the code. The actual data and the check bits represent the end of a long codeword which begins with zeros. As the effect of inputting zeros to the check word circuit during a write is to cause no change, puncturing the code on writing requires no special action. On reading, by a similar argument, the syndrome generated will be as if the whole codeword had been recorded, except that the leading zeros are, of course, error-free, since they were not recorded. Thus the shift count which is arrived at when the burst appears represents the bit count from the beginning of the codeword, not from the beginning of the real data. In practice, it is only necessary to employ an additional shift counter to count the number of leading zeros which were not recorded. When it overflows it enables a second shift counter to count shifts from the beginning of the data. The block diagram of such a system is shown in Figure 4.26. There are two outputs from the circuit: first the error-burst pattern, which will contain a one for every bit in error; and second the location of the start of the burst in bits from the beginning of the block.

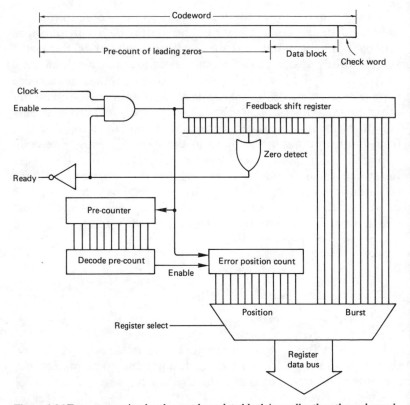

Figure 4.26 Error-correction hardware where data block is smaller than the codeword length. When a non-zero syndrome is detected after a read, the leading zeros in the codeword which precede the data are counted by the pre-counter. When the pre-count satisfies the decoder, the error-position counter is enabled, which gives error position relative to the start of data when zero condition is detected. This disables the shifting and raises the ready bit

An alternative is to construct a slightly different version of the twisted-ring counter for syndrome shifting, which runs through the Galois field backwards. With punctured codes this will perform correction faster. An even faster correction in Fire code can be obtained using the so called Chinese-remainder theorem. Instead of dividing the codeword by the full polynomial, it is simultaneously divided by the factors of the polynomial instead. If there is an error the burst-pattern syndrome is shifted first to locate the burst pattern at the end of the register. The registers containing the other factors can then be shifted until their contents are the same as the burst pattern, when the number of shifts each needs can be used to find the burst position. In addition to allowing the use of conveniently sized blocks, puncturing a code can also be employed to decrease the probabilities of undetected error or miscorrection. Clearly, if part of a codeword is not recorded it cannot contain errors!

While Fire code was discovered at about the same time as the superior Reed–Solomon codes, it was dominant in disk drives until recently because it is so much easier to implement in circuitry. All that is needed is a handful of XOR gates, latches and counters or, more recently, one chip.

4.15 B-adjacent code

In the B-adjacent code, used in consumer digital audio adaptors conforming to the EIAJ format, two bursts can be corrected. The mechanism is shown in Figure 4.27, and operates as follows.

Six words of 14 bits, A–F, are made into a codeword by the addition of two redundancy words, P and Q. The P word is a simple exclusive–OR sum of A–F, but the calculation of Q is more complex. The circuit of Figure 4.27(a) is supplied with each data word in turn and clocked, so that after six clocks the Q word has been calculated. The effect of the circuit of Figure 4.27(a) is actually to perform the matrix transform of Figure 4.27(b). If the transform is given by T, then Q will be given by

$$Q = T^6A \oplus T^5B \oplus T^4C \oplus T^3D \oplus T^2E \oplus TF$$

where $\oplus$ is modulo-2 addition.

The words A–F and P and Q form a codeword and are recorded. On replay, a separate mechanism determines which symbols in the codeword contain errors by the erasure method noted earlier in this chapter. For the purposes of this discussion it is assumed that words A and C are in error. The readback words are all fed into a similar circuit to the encoder. Since the codeword has the characteristic that it gives zero remainder when fed into the check circuit, it follows that the syndrome left in the check circuit in the case of an error is a function of the error alone. If words A and C are in error, the P section of the syndrome SP will be the exclusive–OR of the two errors,

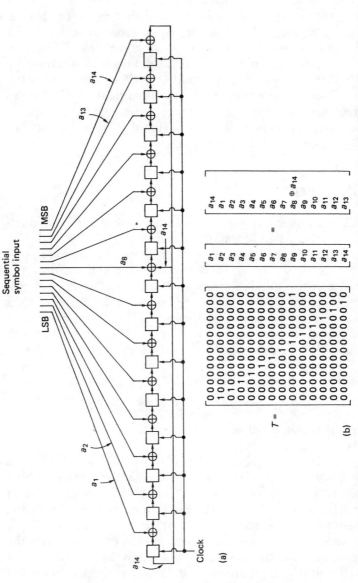

Figure 4.27 B-adjacent encoding; the circuit at (a) is presented with the input symbols sequentially, and each one is clocked. The feedback connections cause the circuit to execute the transform T shown in (b) at each clock. After several clocks, the register will contain the sum of each symbol multiplied by successively higher powers of T

EA $\oplus$ EC. The Q section of the syndrome SQ will be the exclusive–OR sum of the A word error multiplied by the sixth power of the transform T and the C word error multiplied by the fourth power of T:

$$SP = EA \oplus EC \tag{4.1}$$

$$SQ = T^6EA \oplus T^4EC \tag{4.2}$$

Dividing through Eqn (4.2) by T^4 gives

$$T^{-4}SQ = T^2EA \oplus EC \tag{4.3}$$

Adding SP to both sides of Eqn (4.3) gives

$$SP \oplus T^{-4}SQ = T^2EA \oplus EC \oplus SP$$

But SP = EA $\oplus$ EC, therefore

$$SP \oplus T^{-4}SQ = T^2EA \oplus EC \oplus EA \oplus EC$$

$$= T^2EA \oplus EA$$

$$= (1 \oplus T^2)EA$$

Therefore:

$$EA = \frac{SP \oplus T^{-4}\,SQ}{1 \oplus T^2}$$

and EC follows from Eqn (4.1).

It is thus only necessary to process the Q syndrome in a reverse transform according to the positions of the errors in the codeword in order to correct both errors.

4.16 Reed–Solomon codes

In the B-adjacent code, data are assembled into words for the purpose of burst correction. This is implicit in the operation of the Reed–Solomon codes.

The concept of the Galois field has been introduced earlier in this chapter in conjunction with Fire code. In Fire code, the error-burst pattern becomes one state of a Galois field, the syndrome becomes another, but the data bits are all still individually treated. In the Reed–Solomon codes, data bits are assembled into words, or symbols, which become elements of the

Galois field upon which the code is based. The number of bits in the symbol determines the size of the Galois field and hence the number of symbols in the codeword. A symbol size of eight is commonly used because it fits in conveniently with both 16-bit audio samples, eight-bit video samples and byte-oriented computers. It is also highly appropriate for the Compact Disc and RDAT since the EFM and 8/10 channel codes are group codes which can suffer up to eight bits in error if a single channel bit is corrupted. A Galois field with eight-bit symbols has a maximum sequence length of $2^8 - 1 = 255$. As each symbol contains eight bits, the code word will be $255 \times 8 = 2040$ bits long.

As further examples, five-bit symbols could be used to form a codeword 31 symbols long and three-bit symbols would form a codeword seven symbols long. This latter size is small enough to permit some worked examples and will be used further here.

In Section 4.12 it was shown that the circuit of Figure 4.16 generated a Galois field when clocked with no input. The primitive element a will do this when raised to sequential powers. In Reed–Solomon coding, each symbol will be multiplied by some power of such a primitive element. It is necessary to construct hardware which will perform this multiplication. Figure 4.28 shows some examples, and Table 4.1 shows that a truth table can be drawn up for a Galois field multiplier by simply adding the powers of the inputs.

For example

$$a^2 = 100, \ a^3 = 011, \text{ so } 100 \times 011 = a^5 = 111$$

Note that the results of a Galois multiplication are quite different from binary multiplication. Because all products must be elements of the field, sums of powers which exceed seven wrap around by having seven subtracted:

$$a^5 \times a^6 = a^{11} = a^4 = 110$$

It has been stated that the effect of an error is to add an error polynomial to the message polynomial. The number of terms in the error polynomial is the same as the number of errors in the codeword. In a simple CRC system the effect of the error is detected by ensuring that the codeword can be divided by a polynomial. In the Reed–Solomon codes several errors can be isolated by ensuring that the codeword will divide by a number

Table 4.1 The truth table for Galois field multiplication of GF (2^3). $F(x) = x^3 + x + 1$. Primitive element $a = 010$

Element: Bits:	0 000	a 010	a^2 100	a^3 011	a^4 110	a^5 111	a^6 101	$a^7 = 1$ 001
0 000	0 000	0 000	0 000	0 000	0 000	0 000	0 000	0 000
a 010	0 000	a^2 100	a^3 011	a^4 110	a^5 111	a^6 101	1 001	a 010
a^2 100	0 000	a^3 011	a^4 110	a^5 111	a^6 101	1 001	a 010	a^2 100
a^3 011	0 000	a^4 110	a^5 111	a^6 101	1 001	a 010	a^2 100	a^3 011
a^4 110	0 000	a^5 111	a^6 101	1 001	a 010	a^2 100	a^3 011	a^4 110
a^5 111	0 000	a^6 101	1 001	a 010	a^2 100	a^3 011	a^4 110	a^5 111
a^6 101	0 000	1 001	a 010	a^2 100	a^3 011	a^4 110	a^5 111	a^6 101
$a^7 = 1$ 001	0 000	a 010	a^2 100	a^3 011	a^4 110	a^5 111	a^6 101	1 001

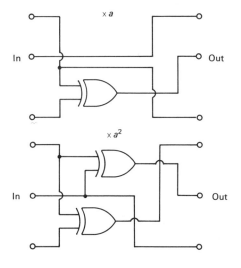

Figure 4.28 Some examples of GF multiplier circuits

Table 4.2 When the position of errors is known by some other means, two errors can be corrected for the same amount of redundancy. The technique is to set the symbols in error to zero, as shown, and calculate what they should have been. This gives the name of erasure correction to the system

A	101	$a^7A =$	101	
B	100	$a^6B =$	010	$S_0 = C \oplus D$
C	000	$a^5C =$	000	$S_1 = a^5 C \oplus a^4 D$
D	000	$a^4D =$	000	
E	111	$a^3E =$	010	
P	100	$a^2P =$	110	
Q	100	$a Q =$	011	
S_0	$= 110$	$S_1 =$	000	

$$S_1 = a^5 S_0 \oplus a^5 D \oplus a^4 D = a^5 S_0 \oplus D$$

$$\therefore D = S_1 \oplus a^5 S_0 = 000 \oplus 100 = \underline{100}$$

$$S_1 = a^5 C \oplus a^4 C \oplus a^4 S_0 = C \oplus a^4 S_0$$

$$\therefore C = S_1 \oplus a^4 S_0 = 000 \oplus 010 = \underline{010}$$

of first-order polynomials. If it is proposed to correct for a number of symbols in error given by t, the codeword must be divisible by $2t$ different polynomials of the form $(x + a^n)$ where n takes all values up to $2t$; a is the primitive element discussed earlier.

Figure 4.29, Figure 4.30 and Table 4.2 show some examples of Reed–Solomon coding processes. The Galois field of Figure 4.16 has been used, and the primitive element $a = 010$ from Table 4.1 will be used. Five symbols of three bits each, A–E, are the data, and two redundant symbols, P and Q, will be used because this simple example will locate and correct only a single symbol in error. It does not matter, however, how many bits in the symbol are in error.

The two check symbols are solutions to the following equations:

$$A \oplus B \oplus C \oplus D \oplus E \oplus P \oplus Q = 0$$

$$a^7A \oplus a^6B \oplus a^5C \oplus a^4D \oplus a^3E \oplus a^2P \oplus aQ = 0$$

By some tedious mathematics, which are shown for reference in Appendix 4.1, it is possible to derive the following expressions which must be used to calculate P and Q from the data in order to satisfy the above equations. These are

$$P = a^6A + aB + a^2C + a^5D + a^3E$$

$$Q = a^2A + a^3B + a^6C + a^4D + aE$$

In Figure 4.29 the redundant symbols have been calculated. In order to calculate P the symbol A is multiplied by a^6 according to Table 4.1; B is multiplied by a, and so on, and the products are added modulo-2. A similar process is used to calculate Q. The entire codeword now exists and can be recorded. Figure 4.29 also demonstrates that the codeword satisfies the checking equations.

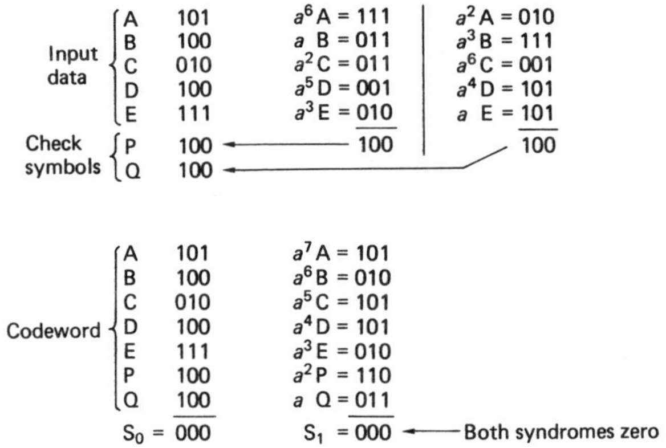

Input data {	A	101	a^6 A = 111	a^2 A = 010
	B	100	a B = 011	a^3 B = 111
	C	010	a^2 C = 011	a^6 C = 001
	D	100	a^5 D = 001	a^4 D = 101
	E	111	a^3 E = 010	a E = 101
Check symbols {	P	100 ←	———— 100	↗ 100
	Q	100 ←		

Codeword {	A	101	a^7 A = 101
	B	100	a^6 B = 010
	C	010	a^5 C = 101
	D	100	a^4 D = 101
	E	111	a^3 E = 010
	P	100	a^2 P = 110
	Q	100	a Q = 011
	S_0 =	$\overline{000}$	S_1 = $\overline{000}$ ← Both syndromes zero

Figure 4.29 Five data symbols A–E are used as terms in the generator polynomials derived in Appendix 4.1 to calculate two redundant symbols P and Q. An example is shown at the top. Below is the result of using the codeword symbols A–Q as terms in the checking polynomials. As there is no error, both syndromes as zero

Upon replaying the information two checks must be made on the received message to see if it is a codeword. This is done by calculating syndromes using the following expressions, where the (′) implies the received symbol which is not necessarily correct

$$S_0 = A' \oplus B' \oplus C' \oplus D' \oplus E' \oplus P' \oplus Q'$$
(This is in fact a simple parity check.)

$$S^1 = a^7A' \oplus a^6B' \oplus a^5C' \oplus a^4D' \oplus a^3E' \oplus a^2P' \oplus aQ'$$

7	A	101	$a^7 A = 101$	
6	B	100	$a^6 B = 010$	$\dfrac{S_1}{S_0} = \dfrac{a^4}{1} = a^4$
5	C	010	$a^5 C = 101$	
4	D'	101	$a^4 D' = 011$ ⟵	$k = 4$
3	E	111	$a^3 E = 010$	
2	P	100	$a^2 P = 110$	$D' + S_0 = 101 + 001$
1	Q	100	$a\, Q = 011$	$D = 100$
	$S_0 =$	$\overline{001}$	$S_1 = \overline{110}$	

7	A	101	$a^7 A = 101$	
6	B	100	$a^6 B = 010$	$\dfrac{S_1}{S_0} = \dfrac{1}{a^2} = \dfrac{1}{a^2} \times \dfrac{a^5}{a^5} = a^5$
5	C'	110	$a^5 C = 100$ ⟵	
4	D	100	$a^4 D = 101$	$k = 5$
3	E	111	$a^3 E = 010$	
2	P	100	$a^2 P = 110$	$C' + S_0 = 110 + 100$
1	Q	100	$a\, Q = 011$	$C = 010$
	$S_0 =$	$\overline{100}$	$S_1 = \overline{001}$	

7	A'	111	$a^7 A = 111$	
6	B	100	$a^6 B = 010$	$\dfrac{S_1}{S_0} = \dfrac{a}{a} = 001 = a^7$
5	C	010	$a^5 C = 101$	
4	D	100	$a^4 D = 101$	$k \doteq 7$
3	E	111	$a^3 E = 010$	
2	P	100	$a^2 P = 110$	$A' + S_0 = 111 + 010$
1	Q	100	$a\, Q = 011$	$A = 101$
	$S_0 =$	$\overline{010}$	$S_1 = \overline{010}$	

Figure 4.30 Three examples of error location and correction. The number of bits in error in a symbol is irrelevant; if all three were wrong, S_0 would be 111, but correction is still possible

In Figure 4.30 three examples of errors are given, where the erroneous symbol is marked with a dash. As there has been an error the syndromes S_0 and S_1 will not be zero. The syndrome calculation is performed using the Table 4.1 as before.

The parity syndrome S_0 determines the error bit pattern, and the syndrome S_1 is the same error bit pattern but it has been raised to a different power of a dependent on the position of the error symbol in the block. If the position of the error is in symbol k, then

$$S_0 \times a^k = S_1$$

Hence

$$a^k = \frac{S_1}{S_0}$$

The error symbol can be located by multiplying S_0 by various powers of a (which is the same as multiplying by successive elements of the Galois field) until the product is the same as S_1.

The power of a necessary is known as the locator because it gives the position of the error. The process of finding the error position by experiment is known as a Chien search [9]. Once the locator has identified the erroneous symbol, the correct value is obtained by adding S_0 (the corrector) to it.

In the examples of Figure 4.30 two redundant symbols have been used to locate and correct one error symbol. If the positions of errors are known by some separate mechanism (see crossinterleaving, Section 4.18), the number of symbols which can be corrected is equal to the number of redundant symbols. In Table 4.2 two errors have taken place and it is known that they are in symbols C and D. Since S_0 is a simple parity check it will reflect the modulo-2 sum of the two errors. Hence

$$S_0 = EC \oplus ED$$

The two errors will have been multiplied by different powers in S_1, such that

$$S_1 = a^5 EC \oplus a^4 ED$$

It is possible to solve these two equations, as shown in the diagram, to find EA and EB, and the correct value of the symbol will be obtained by adding these correctors to the erroneous values. It is, however, easier to set the values of the symbols in error to zero and the correct values are then found more simply, as shown in Table 4.2. This setting of symbols to zero gives rise to the term erasure.

The necessary circuitry for encoding the examples given is shown in Figure 4.31. The P and Q redundancy is computed using suitable Galois field multipliers to obtain the necessary powers of the primitive element according to Table 4.1. Figure 4.32 shows the circuitry for calculating the syndromes. The S_0 circuit is a simple parity checker which produces the modulo-2 sum of all symbols fed to it. The S_1 circuit is more subtle because it contains a Galois field multiplier in a feedback loop, such that early symbols fed in are raised to higher powers than later symbols because they have been recirculated through the GF multiplier more often. It is possible to compare the operation of these circuits with the examples of Figure 4.29, Figure 4.30 and Table 4.2 to confirm that the same results are obtained.

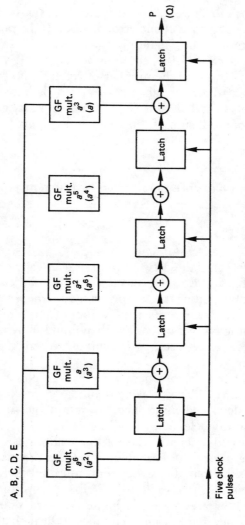

Figure 4.31 If the five data symbols of Figures **4.29** and **4.30** and Table 4.2 are supplied to this circuit in sequence, after five clocks, one of the check symbols will appear at the output. Terms without brackets will calculate P, bracketed terms calculate Q

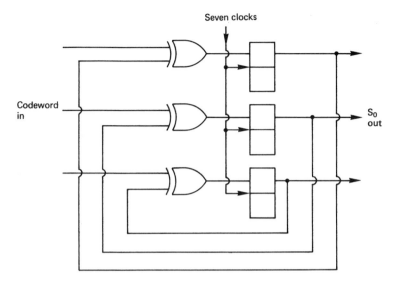

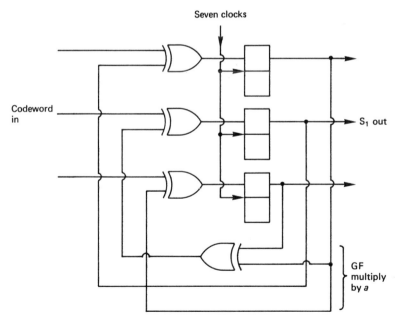

Figure 4.32 Circuits for parallel calculation of syndromes S_0, S_1. S_0 is a simple parity check. S_1 has a GF multiplication by a in the feedback, so that A is multiplied by a^7, B is multiplied by a^6, etc., and all are summed to give S_1

Where two symbols are to be corrected without the help of erasure pointers, four redundant symbols are necessary and the codeword polynomial must then be divisible by

$$(x + a^0)(x + a^1)(x + a^2)(x + a^3)$$

Upon receipt of the message, four syndromes must be calculated and the two error patterns and their positions are determined by solving four simultaneous equations. This generally requires an iterative procedure and a number of algorithms have been developed for the purpose [10–12]. Clearly, a double-error-correcting R–S code will be capable of four-symbol correction if erasure pointers are available. Such techniques are very powerful because the amount of overhead necessary can be made quite small without sacrificing output error rate. The D-1 and D-2 digital video formats, Compact Disc, RDAT and the Mitsubishi stationary-head digital audio formats use erasure techniques with Reed–Solomon coding extensively, and a discussion of the details can be found in Chapter 5. The primitive polynomial commonly used with GF (256) is

$$x^8 + x^4 + x^3 + x^2 + 1$$

The larger Galois fields require less redundancy but the computational problem increases. LSI chips have been developed specifically for R–S decoding for CD and for other formats [13].

4.17 Interleaving

The concept of bit interleaving was introduced in connection with a single-bit correcting code to allow it to correct small bursts. With burst-correcting codes such as Reed–Solomon, bit interleave is unnecessary. In most channels, particularly high density recording channels used for digital audio, the burst size may be many bytes rather than bits, and to rely on a cyclic code alone to correct such errors would require a lot of redundancy. The solution in this case is to employ word interleaving, as shown in Figure 4.33(a). Several codewords are encoded from input data, but these are not recorded in the order they were input, but are physically reordered in the channel so that a real burst error is split into smaller bursts in several codewords. The

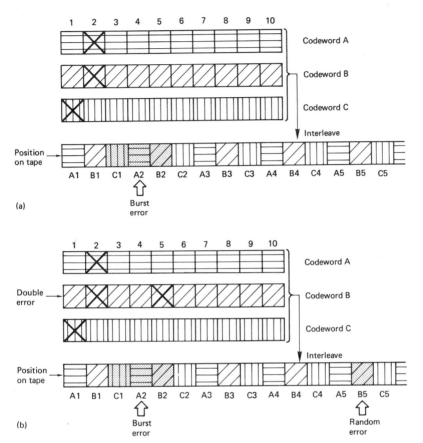

Figure 4.33 At (a), interleave controls the size of burst errors in individual codewords, but at (b) the system falls down when a random error occurs adjacent to a burst

size of the burst seen by each codeword is now determined primarily by the parameters of the interleave, and Figure 4.34 shows that the probability of occurrence of bursts with respect to the burst length in a given codeword is modified. The number of bits in the interleave word can be made equal to the burst-correcting ability of the code in the knowledge that it will be exceeded only very infrequently.

There are a number of different ways in which interleaving can be performed. Figure 4.35 shows that in block interleaving words are reordered within blocks which are themselves in the correct order. This approach is attractive in PCM adaptors for

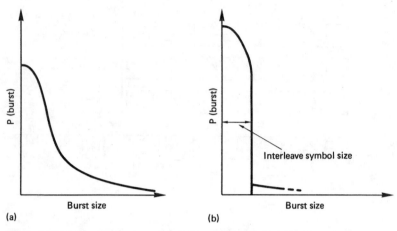

Figure 4.34 (a) The distribution of burst sizes might look like this. (b) Following interleave, the burst size within a codeword is controlled to that of the interleave symbol size, except for gross errors which have low probability

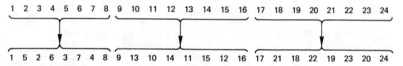

Figure 4.35 In block interleaving, data are scrambled within blocks which are themselves in the correct order

use with video cassette recorders, such as the Sony PCM-1610/ 1630, because the blocks fit into the frame structure of the television waveform and editing is easy. The block interleave is achieved by writing samples into a memory in sequential address locations from a counter and reading the memory with non-sequential addresses from a sequencer. The effect is to convert a one-dimensional sequence of samples into a two-dimensional structure having rows and columns.

Figure 4.36 shows that in convolutional interleaving the interleave process is endless. Samples are assembled into short blocks and then each sample is individually delayed by an amount proportional to the position in the block. Clearly, rows cannot be practically assembled in an endless process because they would be infinitely long, so convolutional interleave produces diagonal codewords. It is possible for a convolutional interleave to continue from track to track in rotary-head systems.

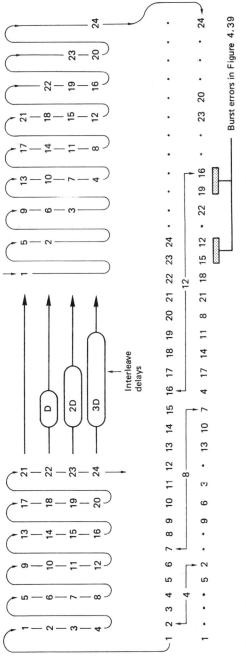

133

Figure 4.36 In convolutional interleaving, samples are formed into a rectangular array, which is sheared by subjecting each row to a different delay. The sheared array is read in vertical columns to provide the interleaved output. In this example, samples will be found at 4, 8 and 12 places away from their original order

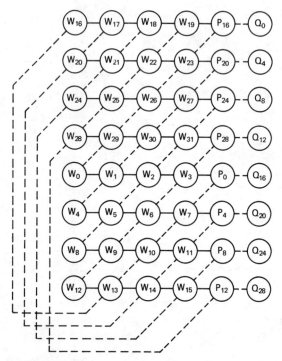

Figure 4.37 In block-completed convolutional interleave some diagonal codewords wrap around the end of the block. This requires a large memory and causes a longer deinterleaving delay

Convolutional interleave requires some caution in editing and this will be discussed later in the chapter. A combination of the two techniques mentioned above is shown in Figure 4.37, where a convolutional code is made to have finite size by making it into a loop. This is known as a block-completed convolutional code and is found in the digital audio blocks of the Video 8 format and in JVC PCM adaptors. The effect of the interleave can be maintained in block-completed interleave provided the block is large enough compared to the interleave parameters, but this requires a large interleave memory.

The above interleaves assume that a single one-dimensional channel is available for the information. In the Compact Disc this is true as there is only one laser beam and a continuous track, but in stationary-head magnetic tape recorders there can be several channels available using a multitrack head. It is

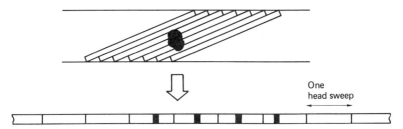

Figure 4.38 Helical-scan recorders produce a form of mechanical interleaving, because one large defect on the medium becomes distributed over several head sweeps

possible to interleave samples by distributing them across many tracks because the average dropout will only affect one or two tracks. This technique is used in the Mitsubishi digital audio recorders conforming to the PD (ProDigi) format, and in the medium- and slow-speed versions of the DASH format. Rotary-head recorders naturally interleave spatially on the tape. Figure 4.38 shows that a single large tape defect becomes a series of small defects owing to the geometry of helical scanning.

4.18 Crossinterleaving

In the presence of burst errors alone, the system of interleaving works very well but it is known that in many channels there are also uncorrelated errors of a few bits due to noise. Figure 4.33(b) shows that a noise error in the vicinity of a burst error will cause two errors in one codeword, which may not be correctable. The solution to this problem is to use a system where codewords are formed both before and after the interleave process. In block interleaving, this results in a product code, whereas in convolutional interleaving the result is known as crossinterleaving [14]. Many of the characteristics of these systems are similar. Figure 4.39(a) shows a crossinterleave system where several errors have taken place. In one row, there are two errors, which are beyond the power of the codeword to correct, and on two diagonals the same is true. However, if a diagonal has two errors, a row will generally only have one. This one error can be corrected, which means that one of the two errors in the diagonal disappears and so the diagonal codeword can correct it. This

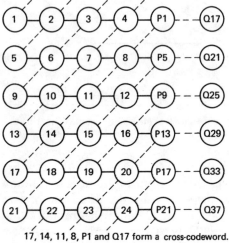

1, 2, 3, 4 and P1 form a codeword

17, 14, 11, 8, P1 and Q17 form a cross-codeword.

(a)

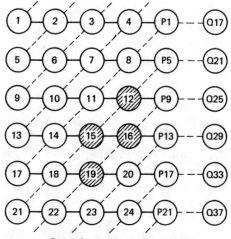

Correction sequence
P9 corrects 12, which enables Q21 to correct 15.
With 15 correct, P13 corrects 16.
P17 corrects 19.

(b)

Figure 4.39 (a) in crossinterleaving, codewords are formed on data before interleaving (1, 2, 3, 4, P1), and after convolutional interleaving (21, 18, 15, 12, P5, Q21). Compare with Figure **4.36**. (b) Multiple errors in one codeword will become single errors in another. If the sequence shown is followed, then all the errors can be corrected. In this example, error samples 12, 15, 16 and 19 are due to two bursts in the convolutional interleave of Figure **4.36**

then means that there will be only one error in the next row, and so on. Random errors in the vicinity of bursts can now be corrected.

In fact, the power of crossinterleaving and product codes goes beyond the ability to deal with real-life errors. The fact that there is a two-dimensional structure allows the position of an error to be discovered because it will be at the intersection of two codewords. If the position of the error can be established geometrically, then it is not necessary to find it by using a code which needs redundancy. The overhead required for a product code is actually less than any other system for a given performance because the detection of an error in one codeword before deinterleave can be used to generate erasure pointers which help a further codeword after deinterleave. The combination of codewords with interleaving in several dimensions yields an error-protection strategy which is truly synergistic in that the end result is more powerful than the sum of the parts. Needless to say, the technique is used extensively in digital recording systems.

4.19 Editing interleaved recordings

The presence of a convolutional interleave means that editing has to be undertaken with care. If a new recording is joined to a previous recording the diagonal codewords over a constraint length near the edit point will be destroyed and the correction power of the system will be limited. Editing must be a read–modify–write process to avoid the destruction of codewords. If editing has to be done in real time, as is often the case with audio recorders, there is only one approach to a convolutional interleave and this is shown in Figure 4.40. Prior to the edit point the replay head signal is deinterleaved and this signal is fed to the record channel. The record channel reinterleaves the samples and produces a signal which will, after some time, be the same as that already on the tape. By this time the original recording will have travelled some distance and a second head is positioned that distance after the playback head. At a block boundary the record amplifier is enabled and the record head will then be rerecording what is already on the tape. The crossfader can now be faded over to the new material, and

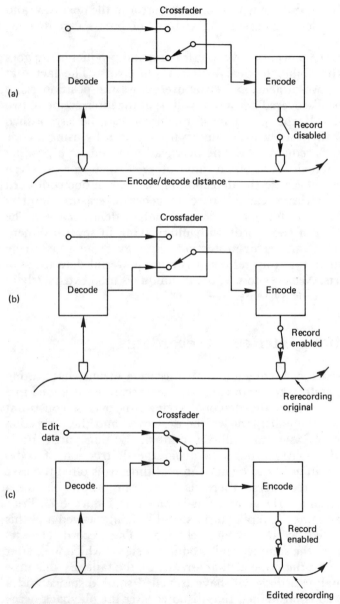

Figure 4.40 Editing a convolutionally interleaved recording. (a) Existing recording is decoded and re-encoded. After some time, record can be enabled at (b) when the existing tape pattern is being rerecorded. The crossfader can then be operated, resulting (c) in an interleaved edit on the tape

the interleaved crossfade will be recorded, followed by the new material. All recorders using interleave must adopt this technique and it is often implemented by having extra heads as shown. In stationary-head recorders this is no problem. In rotary head recorders the extra heads must be accommodated on the drum. This method is adopted in the D-1 and D-2 formats.

In stationary-head formats it is often necessary to support tape-cut editing, which requires special techniques for satisfactory results. This subject will be treated in Chapter 5.

Appendix 4.1 Calculation for Reed–Solomon generator polynomials

For a Reed–Solomon codeword over $GF(2^3)$, there will be seven three-bit symbols. For location and correction of one symbol, there must be two redundant symbols P and Q, leaving A–E for data.

The following expressions must be true, where a is the primitive element of $x^3 + x + 1$ and + is XOR throughout:

$$A + B + C + D + E + P + Q = 0 \tag{1}$$
$$a^7A + a^6B + a^5C + a^4D + a^3E + a^2P + aQ = 0 \tag{2}$$

Dividing eq. (2) by a:

$$a^6A + a^5B + a^4C + a^3D + a^2E + aP + Q = 0 = A + B + C + D + E + P + Q$$

Cancelling Q, and collecting terms:

$$(a^6 + 1)A + (a^5 + 1) B + (a^4 + 1) C + (a^3 + 1) D + (a^2 + 1) E = (a +)P$$

Using Table 7.1 to calculate $(a^n + 1)$, e.g. $a^6 + 1 = 101 + 001 = 100 = a^2$

$$a^2A + a^4B + a^5C + aD + a^6E = a^3P$$
$$a^6A + aB + a^2C + a^5D + a^3E = P \tag{3}$$

Multiply eq. (1) by a^2 and equating to eq. (2):

$$a^2A + a^2B + a^2C + a^2D + a^2E + a^2P + a^2Q = 0 = a^7A + a^6B + a^5C + a^4D + a^3E + a^2P + aQ$$

Cancelling a^2P and collecting terms (remember $a^2 + a^2 = 0$):

$$(a^7 + a^2)A + (a^6 + a^2)B + (a^5 + a^2)C + (a^4 + a^2)D + (a^3 \times a^2)E = (a^2 + a)Q$$

Adding powers according to Table 7.1, e.g. $a^7 + a^2 = 001 + 100 = 101 = a^6$:

$$a^6A + B + a^3C + aD + a^5E = a^4Q$$
$$a^2A + a^3B + a^6C + a^4D + aE = Q$$

References

1. SHANNON, C.E. (1948) A mathematical theory of communication. *Bell System Tech. J.* **27** 379

2. BELLIS, F.A. (1976) A multichannel digital sound recorder. Presented at the Video and Data Recording Conference, Birmingham, England. *IERE Conf. Proc.*, No. 35 123–126

3. HAMMING, R.W. (1950) Error-detecting and error-correcting codes. *Bell System Tech. J.*, **26**, 147–160

4. EDWARDS, A.W.F. (1989) Venn diagrams for many sets. *New Scientist*, **1646**, 51–56

5. PETERSON, W. and BROWN, D. (1961) Cyclic codes for error detection. *Proc. IRE*, 228–235

6. FIRE, P. (1959) A class of multiple-error correcting codes for non-independent errors. *Sylvania Reconnaissance Systems Lab. Report.* RSL-E-2

7. BOSSEN, D.C. (1970) B-adjacent error correction. *IBM J. Res. Dev.,* **14,** 402–408

8. REED, I.S. and SOLOMON, G. (1960) Polynomial codes over certain finite fields. *J. Soc. Indust. Appl. Math.,* **8,** 300–304

9. CHIEN, R.T., CUNNINGHAM, B.D. and OLDHAM, I.B. (1969) Hybrid methods for finding roots of a polynomial – with application to BCH decoding. *IEEE Trans. Inf. Theory.,* **IT-15,** 329–334

10. BERLEKAMP, E.R. (1983) *Algebraic Coding Theory.* New York: McGraw-Hill (1967). Reprint edition: Laguna Hills: Aegean Park Press

11. SUGIYAMA, Y. *et al.* (1976) An erasures and errors decoding algorithm for Goppa codes. *IEEE Trans. Inf. Theory,* **IT 22**

12. PETERSON, W.W. and WELDON, E.J. (1972) *Error Correcting Codes,* 2nd edn, MIT Press

13. ONISHI, K., SUGIYAMA, K., ISHIDA, Y., KUSUNOKI, Y. and YAMAGUCHI, T. (1986) A LSI for Reed–Solomon encoder/decoder. Presented at the 80th Audio Engineering Society Convention (Montreux, 1986)preprint 2316(A4)

14. DOI, T.T., ODAKA, K., FUKUDA, G. and FURUKAWA, S. (1979) Crossinterleave code for error correction of digital audio systems. *J. Audio Eng. Soc.,* **27,** 1028

5

Applications

Previous chapters have dealt primarily with the theory behind coding. In this chapter a number of examples of contemporary formats will be given. These have been chosen mainly for the purposes of explanation, and grow steadily in complexity. It will be seen that the particular application has a considerable effect on the choice of error correction strategy.

5.1 PCM adaptors

If digital data are encoded to resemble a video waveform, which is known as pseudo-video or composite digital, they can be recorded on a fairly standard video recorder. Digital audio recorders have been made using quadruplex video recorders, 1 inch video recorders, U-matic cassette recorders, and the smaller consumer formats. The device needed to format the samples in this way is called a PCM adaptor.

Figure 5.1 shows a block diagram of a PCM adaptor. The unit has five main sections. Central to operation is the sync and timing generation, which produces sync pulses for control of the video waveform generator and locking the video recorder, in addition to producing sampling-rate clocks and timecode. An A to D converter allows a conventional analog audio signal to be recorded, but this can be bypassed if a suitable digital input is available. Similarly, a D to A converter is provided to monitor recordings and this, too, can be bypassed by using the direct

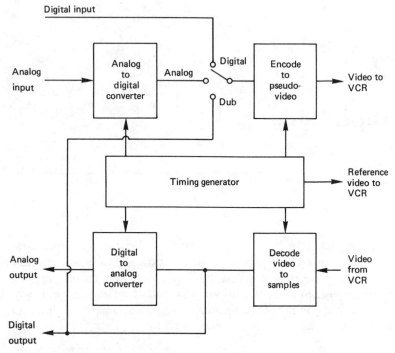

Figure 5.1 Block diagram of PCM adaptor. Note the dub connection needed for producing a digital copy between two VCRs

digital output. Also visible in Figure 5.1 are the encoder and decoder stages which convert between digital sample data and the pseudo-video signal.

An example of this type of unit is the PCM-1610/1630 which was designed by Sony for use with a U-matic video cassette recorder (VCR) specifically for Compact Disc mastering. A matching editor has also been designed.

The Compact Disc format is an international standard and it was desirable for the mastering recorder to adhere to a single format. Thus the PCM-1610 only works in conjunction with a 525/60 monochrome VCR. There is no 625/50 version. Thus even in PAL countries Compact Discs are still mastered on 60 Hz VCRs, which means that the traditional international interchange of recordings can still be achieved. The PCM-1610 was intended for professional use and thus was not intended to be produced in volume. For this reason the format is simple,

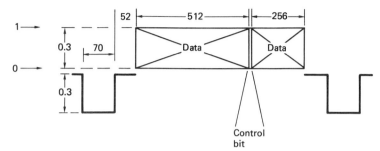

Figure 5.2 Typical line of video from PCM-1610. The control bit conveys the setting of the pre-emphasis switch or the sampling rate depending on position in the frame. The bits are separated using only the timing information in the sync pulses

even crude, because the LSI technology needed to implement more complex formats was not available. This does, however, mean that it makes a good introduction to the subject.

A typical line of pseudo-video is shown in Figure 5.2. The line is divided into bit cells and, within them, black level represents a binary zero, and about 60% of peak white represents binary one. The reason for the restriction to 60% is that most VCRs use non-linear preemphasis and this operating level prevents any distortion due to the preemphasis causing misinterpretation of the pseudo-video. The use of a two-level input to a frequency modulator means that the recording is essentially frequency shift keyed (FSK).

As the video recorder is designed to switch heads during the vertical interval, no samples can be recorded there. In all rotary-head recorders some form of time compression is used to squeeze the samples into the active parts of unblanked lines. This is simply done by reading the samples from a memory at an instantaneous rate which is higher than the sampling rate. Owing to the interruptions of sync pulses the average rate achieved will be the same as the sampling rate. The samples read from the memory must be serialized so that each bit is sent in turn.

It was shown in Chapter 4 that digital recorders use extensive interleaving to combat tape dropout. The PCM-1610 subdivides each video field into seven blocks of 35 lines each, and interleaves samples within the blocks. Figure 5.3 shows that a simple crossword error-correction scheme is used. The input samples 1–3 form a codeword at (a) with a CRC character.

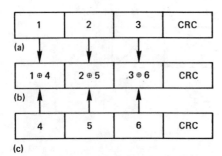

Figure 5.3 In the PCM-1610/1630 format, error correction is via an exclusive-OR term computed from two samples as shown. CRC character detects errors; parity term corrects. Redundancy is high at 100%

Samples 4–6 form another codeword at (c) with a CRC character. The exclusive–OR terms, or modulo-2 sums of the sample pairs shown, form a third codeword with its own CRC character at (b).

If an error occurs the CRC fails but no attempt is made to locate the error by processing the syndrome. All samples in the codeword are presumed faulty. For example, if sample 5 is corrupt, codeword (c) will be in error and samples 4, 5 and 6 are declared to be in error. Sample 4 is obtained by taking the exclusive–OR of sample 1 and the first parity symbol, since 1 XOR (1 XOR 4) = 4. The other two sample values are obtained in a similar way. The system is not very efficient because there is as much redundancy as data, but there is no great need to conserve bandwidth as this is determined by the U-matic format and is plentiful for this application.

Figure 5.4 shows that the interleave over a 35-line period includes a left/right channel interleave and an odd/even sample interleave. The reason for these is that a large burst error damages half of the samples in both audio channels instead of all the samples in one channel. Samples to be recorded are stored in a memory and three passes are made through the memory to encode each 11 ⅔ line segment. The necessary time compression into the active lines is performed with the same memory. The first pass takes odd right samples and even left samples, and produces codewords as in Figure 5.4(a) for 11 ⅔ lines. The next pass takes both right and left samples simultaneously and computes the parity symbols and CRCs for a further 11 ⅔ lines.

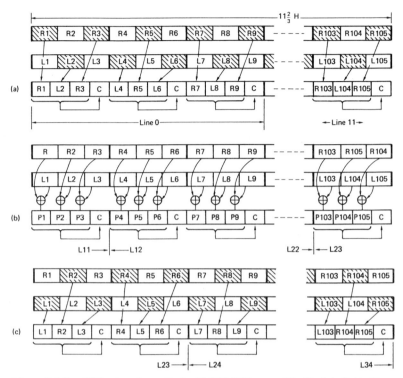

Figure 5.4 One 35-line interleave block of 1610/1630 format. The block is divided into three sections of 11⅔ lines each: two data, one parity. Three passes through the interleave memory are necessary to create the signal structure (a, b, c). The large L/R interleave allows interpolation if dropout exceeds 11⅔ lines

Finally, on the third pass through the memory, even right and odd left samples are made into codewords.

Using this format, dropouts of up to 11 ⅔ lines long are fully correctable since an error of this magnitude will never corrupt more than one of the three related codewords necessary for correction. For example, if line 0 is corrupt, P1, P2 and P3 from the end of line 11, and L1, R2 and L3 from the middle of line 23 are used to correct R1, L2 and R3, and so on. If the dropout continues further, then two codewords of the related threes will be corrupted in some cases, and correction is not then possible. In this case interpolation can be used to conceal the errors. For example, if lines 0–12 are destroyed, L4, R5 and L6 will be uncorrectable (among others) but because of the interleave in line 23, L3 and L5 can be used to recreate L4, R4 and R6 can be used to recreate R5, and L5 and L7 can be used for L6.

If the corruption is more severe, then pairs of samples either side of the wanted sample may not be available and interpolation is impossible. The previous sample will be repeated in this case. Eventually the machine mutes the output to prevent noise. In practice, dropouts are much smaller than the correctable size. The relatively large trackwidth of the U-matic gives a SNR which is much higher than necessary for digital recording, so the random error rate is fairly low and the simple format succeeds. It is not suitable for use with consumer VCRs. A further reason that the 1610 format is restricted to U-matic VCRs is that the timecode is recorded on a linear audio track. This works well with the relatively high linear tape speed of U-matic but is not generally successful on the consumer formats.

Some VCRs have dropout built-in compensators which repeat a section of the previous line to conceal the missing picture information. Such circuits must be disabled when used with PCM adaptors because they interfere with the error-correction mechanism.

5.2 Open reel digital audio recording

The use of digital recording in an audio machine requires techniques which will not be found elsewhere, such as the ability to edit the tape by splicing. This puts peculiar demands on the error-correction and concealment system.

The transport of a digital open reel recorder does not differ in principle from an analog transport, except for the degree of precision necessary to handle narrower tracks on thinner tape.

The control of the capstan is, however, rather different from analog practice. When recording on a blank tape, the capstan turns at constant speed but in all other data transfer modes the capstan is driven at whatever speed is necessary to make the sampling rate correct off tape.

Audio input through an A to D convertor, or a direct digital input form the data source for recordings. Samples are interleaved to resist burst errors and redundancy is added. The data plus redundancy is then assembled into blocks for recording. The blocks are converted to bit serial and fed to an encoder which expresses the data stream as a channel code whose spectrum suits the available channel bandwidth better than the spectrum of raw data. The channel code is used to reverse the record current in the heads, which results in a binary recording on the tape. When the tape is replayed the signal is equalized and used to recreate the write current waveform. This is fed to the data separator, which produces serial data, a separate clock, and identifies the beginning of each of the data blocks on tape. The serial replay data are reassembled into words and undergo the combined processes of deinterleave and error correction. The buffering necessary for deinterleave also removes any wow and flutter. The corrected samples are now available for D to A conversion or the direct digital output. In the case of tape splicing or uncorrectable errors the interpolator will be used and in order to edit the interleaved recordings the crossfader will be used in conjunction with the advanced replay head.

The examples given here are used in the Mitsubishi formats. These are product codes, where codewords are formed across the tape as well as along the tracks. This means that there must be redundant tracks to carry the check symbols which are part of the transverse codewords.

The stereo format of the Mitsubishi X-80 will be discussed first [1]. It is a true stereo format in that samples for both audio channels are combined into a single data structure which is then distributed over all the digital tracks.

In the X-80 format there are eight digital tracks so that one codeword can be formed across the tape. As Figure 5.5 shows, there are also two auxiliary tracks, one for timecode, and one analog audio track for cueing and to assist the location of edit points.

Incoming 16-bit samples from the left and right audio channels are assembled into a rectangular block 14×6, as shown in Figure 5.6. Samples are written into the block such that odd-numbered and even-numbered samples are always on different rows.

The error-correction mechanism uses a product code where detection of the errors and correction are two separate processes.

Figure 5.7 shows how symbols to be recorded are formed into an array. The rows of the sample block are made into codewords by the addition of a 16-bit CRCC at the end of each. These

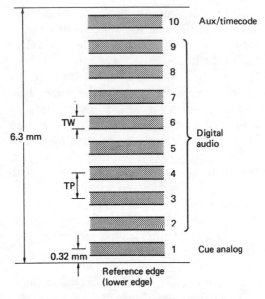

TP = 0.625 mm   TW = 0.305 mm

Figure 5.5 Track dimensions of X-80 stereo format

L1	R1	L7	R7	L13	R13	L19	R19	L25	R25	L31	R31	L37	R37
L2	R2	L8	R8	L14	R14	L20	R20	L26	R26	L32	R32	L38	R38
L3	R3	L9	R9	L15	R15	L21	R21	L27	R27	L33	R33	L39	R39
L4	R4	L10	R10	L16	R16	L22	R22	L28	R28	L34	R34	L40	R40
L5	R5	L11	R11	L17	R17	L23	R23	L29	R29	L35	R35	L41	R41
L6	R6	L12	R12	L18	R18	L24	R24	L30	R30	L36	R36	L42	R42

Figure 5.6 A stereo sample block from X-80 format. There are 42 left-channel and 42 right-channel samples, which gives a block rate of 1200 Hz with a sampling rate of 50.4 kHz

codewords are known as frames. Columns of the block are made into Reed–Solomon codewords by the addition of two symbols of redundancy. At the time this format was designed, LSI technology for Reed–Solomon processing was not cost-effective for professional recorders produced in low volume, and the decoding complexity was minimized by adopting symbols of

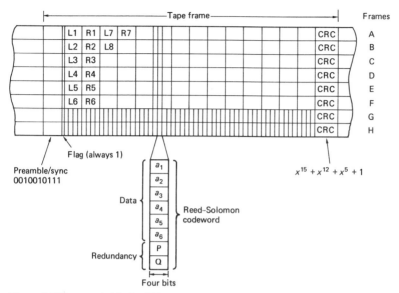

Figure 5.7 The sample block of Figure **5.7** is made into a product code by the addition of redundancy in two dimensions. Horizontally, a CRCC is added for error detection; vertically, two Reed–Solomon symbols are used per column. The R–S symbols are only from bits to simplify processing, and four R–S codewords are needed for one column of samples

only four bits, which meant that it was feasible to use ROM based tables for the Galois arithmetic. As a result, each block is split into 56 columns of four bits each, and each column is made into a Reed–Solomon codeword. The redundancy produced is also made into frames by the addition of a CRCC. Data are written onto the tape by assigning each of the eight frames of the block to a different track. If an error occurs, then the CRC will fail for a given track or frame. The CRC is not intended to locate the error, only to detect it, so the CRC failure simply declares every four-bit symbol in that frame to be in error by attaching an error flag to it. In practice this is not far from the truth since the block size was established by studying the size of typical error bursts. These error flags are used as erasure pointers by the Reed–Solomon code in the columns. Owing to the array structure, a horizontal codeword which is virtually wiped out by an error burst will be converted into single-symbol errors in a large number of different vertical Reed–Solomon codewords. As a Reed–Solomon code can correct as many error symbols as it has redundancy symbols when using erasure, two tape tracks, i.e. two rows of the block, can be in error and correction is still possible.

Actual measurements of tape performance revealed that, in general, if an error was present in one track there was only a minute probability that an error would also be present in an adjacent track [2]. The error-correction system is thus adequate to deal with random errors.

There are two eventualities which cause exceptions to these measurements. When the tape is handled, fingerprints cause two-dimensional dropouts due to spacing loss which affect all tracks simultaneously. Similarly, when the tape is spliced, all tracks are affected at once.

In order to overcome these problems additional interleave is used which is specified in Figure 5.8, where it will be seen that each tape track records data that have been subjected to different delays. The samples which have been heavily delayed on record wil receive less delay on replay, and vice versa. It will also be clear from Figure 5.8 that the odd samples are given rather less delay than the even samples.

The effect of this interleave is that on replay, errors which affect all tracks simultaneously will affect different rows of the array at different times after deinterleave. The effect of fingerprints will thus be to cause a few rows of the array to be corrupted in many different tape frames, rather than many rows being corrupted in a few frames.

When the tape is spliced. errors will occur due to three mechanisms. First, there will be surface contamination due to handling. Second, the beginning and end of the adhesive tape will cause separation loss errors where the flexibility of the tape changes. If the splicing tape has not been trimmed very well, the corner of it may snag the tape guides and cause further error bursts. These will be dealt with as described. Third, the actual splice results in a massive error burst due to distortion of the tape by cutting and the temporary loss of synchronization caused by the arbitrary frame phase jump across the splice. In this case, the odd/even interleave will be used. After deinterleave, the result of a splice will be two error bursts, first in odd samples, then in even. Interpolation can be used as in Figure 5.9, and a crossfade is made when both the old and new recordings are available.

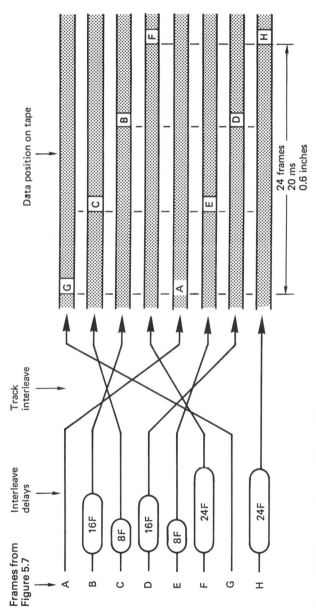

Figure 5.8 The product block of Figure 5.7 is interleaved for recording on tape by the delay system shown here. Further physical interleave is obtained by rearranging the tracks used to record the frames

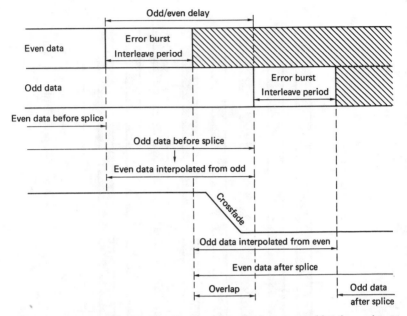

Figure 5.9 Following deinterleave, the effect of a splice is to cause odd and even data to be lost at different times. Interpolation is used to provide the missing samples, and a crossfade is made when both recordings are available in the central overlap

The X-80 used the MFM or Miller channel code developed by Ampex, and was normalized for a linear tape speed of 15 inches per second at 50.4 KHz; MFM was described in Chapter 3.

5.3 ¼ inch ProDigi format

In the ¼ inch ProDigi format, the format of the X-80 is refined and available in three different modes [3,4]. In mode 1, 16-bit 48 KHz stereo at 15 inches per second is suggested for maximum tolerance to splicing. In mode 2 the tape speed is halved by increasing the packing density for applications requiring long recording time. Mode 3 uses 20-bit samples at 15 inches per second so that the entire wordlength of the AES/EBU digital audio interface signal can be recorded. As usual in stationary-head machines, the use of 44.1 kHz or 32 kHz sampling results in a pro-rata reduction in tape speed.

Reference to Figure 5.10 will reveal that there are two analog tracks; a timecode track; and an auxiliary data track. The

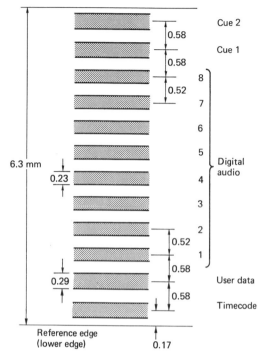

Figure 5.10 Dimensions of ¼ inch ProDigi tracks. Note auxiliary tracks are wider than digital tracks. Track positions are identical to DASH Q

channel code used in ProDigi is known as 2/4M, which is a convolutional run-length-limited code. This has a higher density ratio than MFM and contributes to the higher packing density needed. A description of this code can be found in Chapter 3.

As LSI circuitry for Galois arithmetic was developed for this format the error-correction strategy reflects the increased processing flexibility available [5]. The symbol size in the Reed–Solomon coding is now eight bits and the codewords are now 16 symbols long. The data structure is changed to a convolutional crossinterleave.

Figure 5.11 shows that for 16-bit working (modes 1 and 2) the samples from both audio channels are formed into a four-symbol word, whereas for 20-bit working the word will be five symbols long and one symbol contains four bits from each channel.

These words form the input to the interleave system of Figure 5.12. Odd- and even-numbered samples enter the interleave on

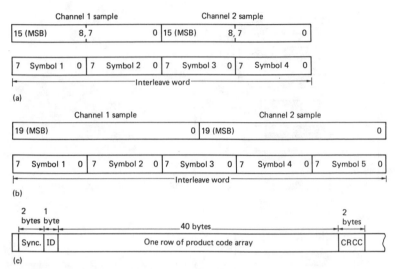

Figure 5.11 (a) In modes 1 and 3, two 16-bit samples from left and right channels are formatted into four bytes for the eight-bit error-correction system. At (b) in mode 2, two 20-bit samples are formatted into five bytes. At (c) one tape frame commences with a sync pattern and ID byte, and contains bytes, which are one row of the product-code array. This can be ten words in 16-bit mode; eight words in 20-bit mode; or 40-bytes of R–S redundancy in the check rows. Frame rate at 48 kHz sampling rate is 800 Hz (modes 1, 2) or 1000 Hz (mode 3)

alternate rows and so the first set of delays cause an odd/even interleave. Following these, 12 symbols are used to compute four redundant Reed–Solomon symbols, making a 16-symbol code-word. A further large odd/even delay is now inserted, which is intended to allow interpolation during splices and gross errors. Following this, the convolutional interleave is implemented with delays which increase proportionately to the symbol position in the codeword, resulting in sets of 16 interleaved symbols. These symbols are then multiplexed into the eight digital tracks on tape. The manner in which this is done is most important. The redundancy symbols are fed to tracks 1 and 8 which are at opposite edges of the tape. If the tape is damaged the greatest corruption is likely at the edges of the tape because they will lose contact with the head if the substrate is distorted. Since the Reed–Solomon redundancy is only necessary if errors are detected in the other tracks, it is recorded nearer the edge of the tape so that the actual samples can be put in the most secure area near the centre.

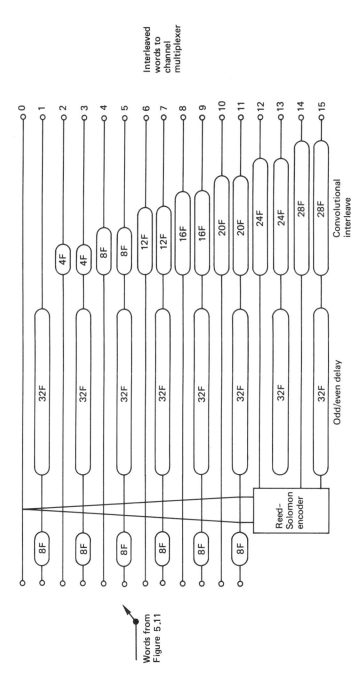

Figure 5.12 Interleave system of ProDigi takes successive words from Figure **5.11** and passes them down 12 different paths. The R–S encoder increases this to 16 paths. The odd/even delay (40 frames total) is for error concealment and splice handling. Convolutional interleave helps error correction of bursts. Delays shown are in frames for modes 1 and 3. For mode 2, double all numbers

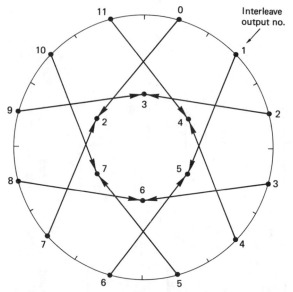

Figure 5.13 The 16 paths of Figure **5.12** are combined into eight tape tracks. The redundancy (12–15) is combined into the outer tracks (1 and 8), and the data (01–1) are multiplexed into the remaining six digital tracks as shown here. By combining odd and even interleave outputs into one tape track, each track is made to have an equal number of odd and even samples

The remaining 12 output channels of the interleave are multiplexed into six digital tracks in accordance with Figure 5.13. It will be noted that pairs of symbols which are separated by constant distance in the interleave are combined into one track. The distance chosen is odd so that each track contains an equal number of odd and even samples which increases the probability that interpolation will be possible. It also means that there is actually an interleave along each track. As an example, if a given even sample enters the first row it is undelayed and fed to track 2. Seven samples later an odd sample passes through the eighth row of the interleave delay and is also fed to track 2. Track 2 thus contains odd and even samples with an interleave between them. Data on each track is assembled into blocks of 40 bytes which represent ten stereo samples of 16 bits or eight stereo samples of 20 bits. An ID or address code is added and the whole is made into a codeword by the addition of a CRCC. This is recorded as a frame on the tape track. The resultant data frame is shown in Figure 5.11(c).

In the event of an error when reading the frame, the CRC will fail and add error flags to all of the symbols in the frame. These will act as erasure pointers for the Reed–Solomon code working after deinterleave. As there are four redundancy symbols in the Reed–Solomon code, four errors in each codeword can be corrected by erasure. The interleave ensures that errors occurring in one place across the tape, such as at the end of the splicing tape, are distributed throughout widely spaced frames. In 20-bit mode, there are less samples in a frame. The packing density has to be raised to raise the frame rate without raising the tape speed. This causes the physical interleave distance to be shorter in 20-bit mode. Figure 5.14 shows the resulting interleave distances on tape for modes 1 and 3.

The slow speed option results in the data density along the tracks being doubled. This would result in the physical interleave distance being halved. It would leave the format twice as prone to damage by dropouts of given dimensions. It is necessary to restore the physical interleave distance by doubling the delays. The resulting interleave is shown in Figure 5.15.

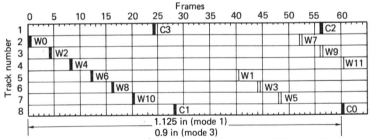

Figure 5.14 Interleave patterns for modes 1 and 3. In mode 3 there are fewer samples in a frame, and interleave becomes physically shorter because the packing density is increased

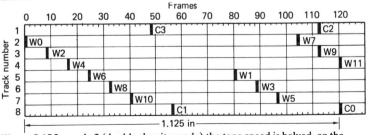

Figure 5.15 In mode 2 (double-density mode) the tape speed is halved, so the interleave extends over twice as many blocks to make the physical interleave of the same size as in mode 1

5.4 Introduction to RDAT

When a video recorder is used as a basis for a digital audio recorder the video bandwidth is already defined and in most cases is much greater than necessary. Furthermore, the SNR of video recorders is much too high for the purposes of storing binary. The result of these factors is that the tape consumption of such a machine will be far higher than necessary. Now that digital audio is becoming established, and markets are seen to exist for large numbers of machines, it is no longer necessary to borrow technology from other disciplines because it is economically viable to design a purpose-built product. The first of this generation of machines is RDAT (rotary-head digital audio tape). By designing for a specific purpose the tape consumption can be made very much smaller than that of a converted video machine. In fact the RDAT format achieves more bits per square inch than any other form of magnetic recorder at the time of writing. The origins of RDAT are in an experimental machine built by Sony [6], but the RDAT format has grown out of that through a process of standardization involving some 80 companies.

The general appearance of the RDAT cassette is shown in Figure 5.16. The overall dimensions are only 73 mm × 54 mm × 10.5 mm, which is rather smaller than the Compact Cassette. The design of the cassette incorporates some improvements over its analog ancestor [7]. As shown in Figure 5.17, the apertures through which the heads access the tape are closed by a hinged door and the hub drive openings are covered by a sliding panel which also locks the door when the cassette is not in the transport. The act of closing the door operates brakes which act on the reel hubs. This results in a cassette which is well sealed against contamination due to handling or storage. The short wavelengths used in digital recording make it more sensitive to spacing loss caused by contamination. As in the Compact Cassette, the tape hubs are flangeless, and the edge guidance of the tape pack is achieved by liner sheets. The flangeless approach allows the hub centres to be closer together for a given length of tape. The cassette has recognition holes in four standard places so that players can automatically determine what type of cassette has been inserted. In addition there is a write-protect (record-lockout) mechanism which is actuated by a small plastic plug sliding between the cassette halves. The end-of-tape condition is detected optically and the leader tape is transparent.

The high coercivity (typically 1480 oersteds) metal powder tape is 3.81 mm wide, the same width as Compact Cassette tape. The standard overall thickness is 13 μm. A striking feature of the metal tape is that the magnetic coating is so thin, at about 3 μm, that the tape appears translucent. The maximum capacity of the cassette is about 60 m.

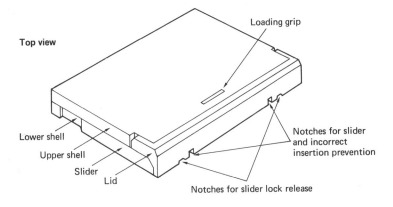

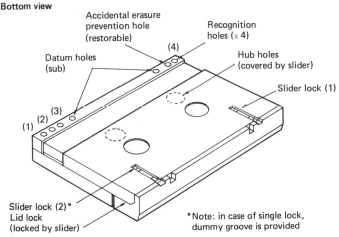

Figure 5.16 Appearance of RDAT cassette. Access to the tape is via a hinged lid, and the hubdrive holes are covered by a sliding panel, affording maximum protection to the tape. Further details of the recognition holes are given in Table 5.1. (Courtesy TDK)

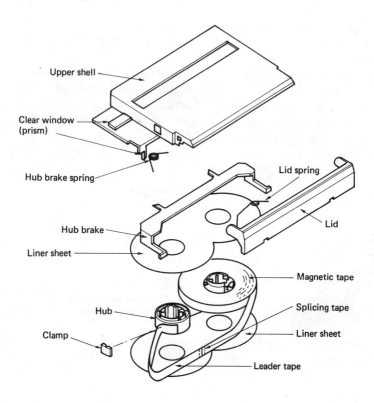

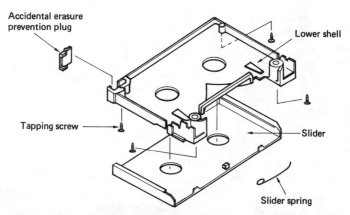

Figure 5.17 Exploded view of RDAT cassette showing intricate construction. When the lid opens, it pulls the ears on the brake plate, releasing the hubs. Note the EOT/BOT sensor prism moulded into the corners of the clear window. (Courtesy TDK)

As its name suggests, the system uses rotary heads, but there is only limited similarity to video recorders. In video recorders each diagonal tape track stores one television field, and the switch from one track to the next takes place during the vertical interval. In a recorder with two heads, one at each side of the drum, it is necessary to wrap the tape rather more than 180 degrees around the drum so that one head begins a new track just before the previous head finishes. This constraint means that the threading mechanism of VCRs is quite complex. In RDAT, threading is simplified because the digital recording does not need to be continuous. Rotary-head digital audio tape extends the technique of time compression used to squeeze continuous samples into intermittent video lines. Blocks of samples to be recorded are written into a memory at the sampling rate, and are read out at a much faster rate when they are to be recorded. In this way the memory contents can be recorded in less time. Figure 5.18 shows that when the samples are time-compressed, recording is no longer continuous but is interrupted by long pauses. During the pauses in recording it is

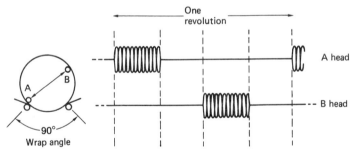

Figure 5.18 The use of time compression reduces the wrap angle necessary, at the expense of raising the frequencies in the channel

not actually necessary for the head to be in contact with the tape and so the angle of wrap of the tape around the drum can be reduced, which makes threading easier. In RDAT the wrap angle is only 90° on the commonest drum size. As the heads are 180° apart, this means that for half the time neither head is in contact with the tape. Figure 5.19 shows that the partial-wrap concept allows the threading mechanism to be very simple indeed. As the cassette is lowered into the transport the pinch roller and several guide pins pass behind the tape. These then

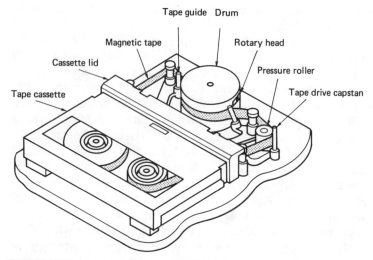

Figure 5.19 The simple mechanism of RDAT. The guides and pressure roller move towards the drum and capstan and threading is complete

simply move towards the capstan and drum and threading is complete. A further advantage of partial wrap is that the friction between the tape and drum is reduced, allowing power saving in portable applications and allowing the tape to be shuttled at high speed without the partial unthreading needed by video-cassettes. In this way the player can read subcode during shuttle to facilitate rapid track access.

The track pattern laid down by the rotary heads is shown in Figure 5.20. The heads rotate at 2000 rev/min in the same direction as tape motion but, because the drum axis is tilted, diagonal tracks 23.5 mm long result at an angle of just over six degrees to the edge. The diameter of the scanner needed is not specified because it is the track pattern geometry which ensures interchange compatibility. For portable machines a small scanner is desirable, whereas for professional use a larger scanner allows additional heads to be fitted for confidence replay and editing.

There are two linear tracks, one at each edge of the tape, where they act as protection for the diagonal tracks against edge damage. Owing to the low linear tape speed the use of these edge tracks is somewhat limited.

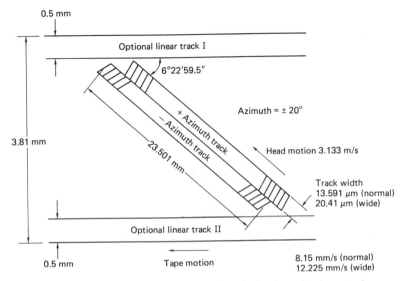

Figure 5.20 The two heads of opposite azimuth angles lay down the above track format. Tape linear speed determines track pitch

Within the standard cassette, several related modes of operation are available. These are compared in Table 5.1. One of the most important modes uses a sampling rate of 48 kHz, with 16-bit two's complement linear quantization. Alongside the audio samples can be carried 273 kilobits/s of subcode and 68.3 kilobits/s of ID coding whose purpose will be explained in due course. With a linear tape speed of 8.15 mm/s, the standard cassette offers 120 min unbroken playing time. All RDAT machines can record and play at 48 kHz. For consumer machines, playback only of prerecorded media is proposed at 44.1 kHz 16-bit two's complement linear quantization. For reasons which will be explained later, prerecorded tapes run at 12.225 mm/s to offer playing time of 80 min. The same subcode and ID rate is offered. The above two modes are mandatory if a machine is to be considered to meet the format. A professional RDAT machine used for CD or prerecorded RDAT mastering will record at 44.1 kHz.

Figure 5.21 shows a block diagram of a typical RDAT recorder. In order to make a recording an analog signal is fed to an input A to D converter or a direct digital input is taken from

164

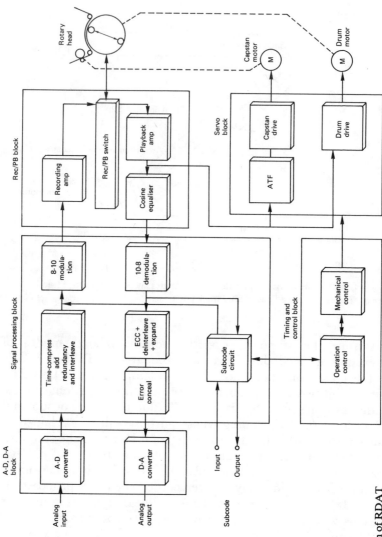

Figure 5.21 Block diagram of RDAT

Table 5.1 The various modes of RDAT contrasted. Mandatory modes are 48 kHz record/play and 44.1 kHz replay. Other modes are optional. Note option 2 runs drum at half-speed for extended playing time

		Record/playback modes			Prerecorded tape playback	
	Mandatory	*Option 1*	*Option 2*	*Option 3*		
Number of channels	2	2	2	4	2	2
Sampling rate (kHz)	48	32	32	32	44.1	44.1
Quantization (bits)	16	16	12 non lin.	12 non lin.	16	16
Tape speed (mm/s)	8.15	8.15	4.075	8.15	8.15	12.225
Subcode rate (kbit/s)	273.1	273.1	136.5	273.1	273.1	273.1
Playing time (13 μm tape)	120	120	240	120	120	80
Drum speed (rev/min)	2000	2000	1000	2000	2000	2000

an AES/EBU interface. The incoming samples are subject to interleaving to reduce the effects of error bursts. Reading the memory at a higher rate than it was written performs the necessary time compression. Additional bytes of redundancy computed from the samples are added to the data stream to permit subsequent error correction. Subcode information is added and the parallel byte structure is converted to serial form and fed to the channel encoder, which produces a recording waveform free of DC and low frequencies. This signal is fed to the heads via a rotary transformer to make the binary recording, which leaves the tape track with a pattern of transitions between the two magnetic states.

On replay the transitions on the tape track induce pulses in the head, which are used to recreate the record current waveform. This is fed to the data separator which converts it to a serial bit stream and a separate clock. The subcode data are routed to the subcode output, and the audio samples are fed into a deinterleave memory which, in addition to time-expanding the recording, functions to remove any wow or flutter due to head-to-tape speed variations. Error correction uses a deeply interleaved product code and is performed partially before and partially after deinterleave. The corrected output samples can be fed to DACs or to a direct digital output.

In order to keep the rotary heads following the very narrow slant tracks, alignment patterns are recorded as well as the data. The automatic track-following system processes the playback signals from these patterns to control the drum and capstan motors. The subcode and ID information can be used by the control logic to drive the tape to any desired location specified by the user.

Like most recent rotary-head machines, RDAT uses azimuth recording. If a channel code is used which has a small low frequency content the failure of the azimuth effect at long wavelengths ceases to be a problem. In the absence of long wavelengths erasure is achieved by overwriting with a new waveform. When overwriting is used in conjunction with azimuth recording the recorded tracks can be made rather narrower than the head pole simply by reducing the linear speed of the tape so that it does not advance so far between sweeps of the rotary heads. In RDAT the head pole is $20.4\,\mu$m wide but the tracks it records are only $13.59\,\mu$m wide. The same head can be used for replay, even though it is 50% wider than the tracks. It was shown in Chapter 2 that the signal-to-crosstalk ratio becomes independent of tracking error over a small range because as the head moves to one side the loss of crosstalk from one adjacent track is balanced by the increase of crosstalk from the track on the opposite side. This phenomenon allows for some loss of track straightness and for the residual error which is present in all track-following servo systems [8].

The track width and the coercivity of the tape largely define the SNR. A track width has been chosen which makes the signal-to-crosstalk ratio dominant in cassettes which are intended for user recording.

Prerecorded tapes are made by contact duplication and this process only works if the coercivity of the copy is less than that of the master. The output from prerecorded tapes at the track width of $13.59\,\mu$m would be too low and would be noise-dominated, which would cause the error rate to rise. The solution to this problem is that in prerecorded tapes the track width is increased to be the same as the head pole. The noise and crosstalk are both reduced in proportion to the reduced output of the medium and the same error rate is achieved as for normal high coercivity tape.

The 50% increase in track width is achieved by raising the

linear tape speed from 8.15 to 12.225 mm/s and so the playing time of a prerecorded cassette falls to 80 min, as opposed to the 120 min of the normal tape. This is not a real restriction since most consumers would not want to purchase so much copyright material at once. Whereas the 20 min playing time per side of vinyl disks was often bemoaned, very few Compact Discs have been released which contain the full 75 min programme.

5.5 Recording in RDAT

The channel code used in RDAT is designed to function well in the presence of crosstalk, to have zero DC component to allow the use of a rotary transformer, and to have a small ratio of maximum and minimum run lengths to ease overwrite erasure. The code used is a group code where eight data bits are represented by ten channel bits, hence the name 8/10. The details of the code are given in Chapter 3.

The basic unit of recording is the sync block shown in Figure 5.22. This consists of the sync pattern, a three-byte header and 32 bytes of data, making 36 bytes in total, or 360 channel bits. The subcode areas each consist of eight of these blocks and the PCM audio area consists of 128 of them. Note that a preamble is

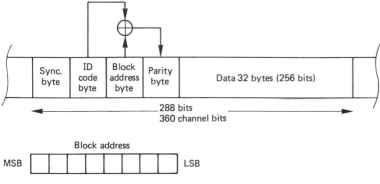

Figure 5.22 One sync block of RDAT; 128 of these are assembled in an unbroken sequence to form the audio segment of a track, with a preamble at the beginning and a postamble after the last block. The seven-bit block address is sufficient to label the 128 blocks uniquely. The block structure of the subcode area is identical, but only eight blocks make a subcode segment

only necessary at the beginning of each area to allow the data separator to phase-lock before the first sync block arrives. Synchronism should be maintained throughout the area but the sync pattern is repeated at the beginning of each sync block in case sync is lost due to dropout.

The first byte of the header contains an ID code which in the PCM audio blocks specifies the sampling rate in use, the number of audio channels, and whether there is a copy-prohibit in the recording. The second byte of the header specifies whether the block is subcode or PCM audio with the first bit. If set, the least significant four bits specify the subcode block address in the track, whereas if it is reset the remaining seven bits specify the PCM audio block address in the track. The final header byte is a parity check and is the exclusive–OR sum of header bytes one and two.

The data format within the tracks can now be explained. The information on the track has three main purposes: PCM audio; subcode data; and ATF patterns. It is necessary to be able to record subcode at a different time from PCM audio in professional machines in order to make mastering tapes for Compact Discs or prerecorded RDAT cassettes. The subcode is placed in separate areas at the beginnings and ends of the tracks. When subcode is recorded on a tape with an existing PCM audio recording the heads have to go into record at just the right time to drop a new subcode area onto the track. This timing is subject to some tolerance and so some leeway is provided by the margin area which precedes the subcode area and the interblock gap (IBG) which follows. Each area has its own preamble and sync pattern so the data separator can lock to each area individually, even though they were recorded at different times or on different machines.

The data interleave is not convolutional, but is block-structured. One pair of tape tracks (one + azimuth and one −azimuth) corresponding to one drum revolution make up an interleave block. Since the drum turns at 2000 rev/min, one revolution takes 30 ms and in this time 1440 samples must be stored for each channel for 48 kHz working.

The first interleave performed is to separate both left- and right-channel samples into odd and even. The right-channel odd samples followed by the left even samples are recorded in the + azimuth track, and the left odd samples followed by the right

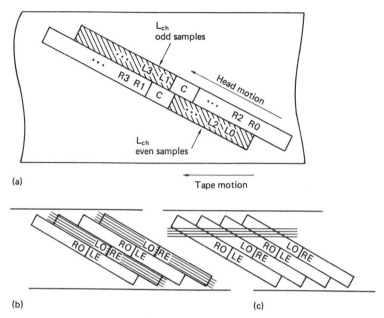

Figure 5.23 (a) Interleave of odd and even samples and left and right channels to permit concealment in case of gross errors. (b) Clogged head loses every other track. Half of the samples of each channel are still available, and interpolation is possible. (c) A linear tape scratch destroys odd samples in both channels. Interpolation is again possible

even samples are recorded in the − azimuth track. Figure 5.23 shows that this interleave allows uncorrectable errors to be concealed by interpolation. At (b) a head becomes clogged and results in every other track having severe errors. The split between right and left samples means that half of the samples in each channel are destroyed instead of every sample in one channel. The missing right even samples can be interpolated from the right odd samples, and the missing left odd samples are interpolated from the left even samples. Figure 5.23(c) shows the effect of a longitudinal tape scratch. A large error burst occurs at the same place in each head sweep. As the positions of left- and right-channel samples are reversed from one track to the next, the errors are again spread between the two channels and interpolation can be used in this case also.

The incoming samples for one head revolution are routed to a pair of memory areas of 4 kbytes capacity, one for each track.

These memories are structured as 128 columns of 32 bytes each. The error correction works with eight-bit symbols and so each sample is divided into high byte and low byte and occupies two locations in memory. Figure 5.24 shows one of the two memories. Incoming samples are written across the memory in rows, with the exception of an area of 24 bytes wide in the centre. Each row of data in the RAM is used as the input to the Reed–Solomon encoder for the outer code. The encoder starts at the left-hand column and then takes a byte from every fourth column, finishing at column 124 with a total of 26 bytes. Six bytes of redundancy are calculated to make a 32-byte outer codeword. The redundant bytes are placed at the top of columns 52, 56, 60, etc. The encoder then makes a second pass through the memory, starting in the second column and taking a byte from every fourth column finishing at column 125. A further six bytes of redundancy are calculated and put into the top of columns 53, 57, 61, and so on. This process is performed four times for each row in the memory, except for the last eight rows where only two passes are necessary because odd-numbered columns have sample bytes only down to row 23. The total number of outer codewords produced is 112.

In order to assemble the data blocks to be recorded the memory is read in columns. Starting at top left, bytes from the 16 even-numbered rows of the first column, and from the first 12 even-numbered rows of the second column, are assembled and fed to the inner encoder. This produces four bytes of redundancy which when added to the 28 bytes of data makes an inner codeword 32 bytes long. Reference to Figure 5.22 will show that this codeword can be accommodated in one sync block. The second sync block is assembled by making a second pass through the first two columns of the memory to read the samples on odd-numbered rows. Four bytes of redundancy are added to these data also. The process then repeats down the next two columns in the memory, and so on until 128 blocks have been written to the tape.

Upon replay the sync blocks will suffer from a combination of random errors and burst errors. The effect of interleaving is that the burst errors will be converted to many single-symbol errors in different outer codewords. As there are four bytes of redundancy in each inner codeword, one or two bytes due to random error can be corrected, which prevents random errors

171

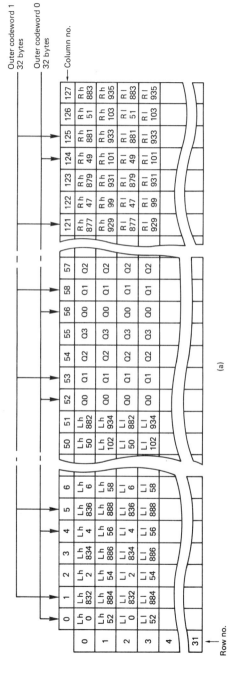

Figure 5.24 (a) Left even/right odd interleave memory. Incoming samples are split into high byte (h) and low byte (l), and written across the memory rows using first the even columns for L 0–830 and R 1–831, then the odd columns for L 832–1438 and R 833–1439. For 44.1 kHz working, the number of samples is reduced from 1440 to 1323, and fewer locations are filled

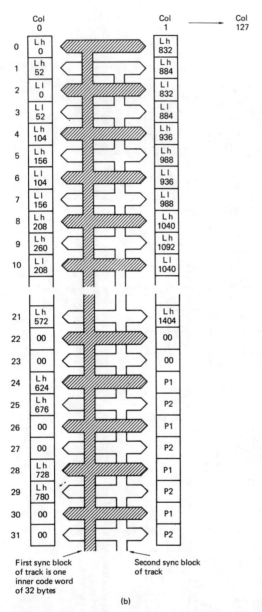

Figure 5.24 (*Cont*) (b) The columns of memory are read out to form inner codewords. First, even bytes from the first two columns make one codeword, which is also one sync block, then odd bytes from the first two columns. As there are 128 columns, there will be 128 sync blocks in one audio segment

impairing the burst-error correction of the outer code. The probability of miscorrection in the inner code is minute for a single-byte error because all four syndromes will agree on the nature of the error, but the probability of miscorrection on a double-byte error is much higher. If two or more bytes are in error in a sync block the inner code will be overwhelmed and can only declare all bytes bad by attaching flags to them as they enter the deinterleave memory. After deinterleave these flags will show up as single-byte errors in many different outer codewords accompanied by error flags. To guard against miscorrections in the inner code the outer code will calculate syndromes even if no error flags are received from the inner code. If two or less bytes in error are detected the outer code will correct them, even though they were due to inner code miscorrections. This can be done with high reliability because the outer code has three-byte correcting power which is never used to the full. If more than two bytes are in error in the outer codeword, the correction process uses the error flags from the inner code to correct up to six bytes in error by erasure.

The reasons behind the devious interleaving process now become clearer. Because of the four-way interleave of the outer code, four entire sync blocks can be destroyed but only one byte will be corrupted in a given outer codeword. As an outer codeword can correct up to six bytes in error by erasure, it follows that a burst error of up to 24 sync blocks could be corrected. This corresponds to a length of track of just over 2.5 mm and is more than enough to cover the tenting effect due to a particle of debris lifting the tape away from the head.

5.6 DDS–RDAT as a data storage medium

When digital audio recording was in its infancy, devices intended for use with computers were adapted for audio applications. The rapid rate of adoption of digital audio has fuelled an impressive acceleration of the technology, with the result that audio devices are now being adapted for computer use. Digital data storage (DDS) is the computer storage derivative of RDAT.

Although the basic principles of digital recording are not changed by the application, many of the performance criteria have to be judged according to different values. Residual errors are unacceptable in computer data, particularly if they are in machine code since this is necessarily a condensed form of data. Data integrity must be such that there will be less than one bit in error in 10^{12} or 10^{15}. In audio data, uncorrected errors result in impulsive noise whose audibility depends upon the significance of the affected bit. Since the sampling rate of digital audio is high with respect to the frequencies which determine intelligibility, there is a lot of redundancy in the data and concealment can be used where simple interpolation can provide a substitute for the erroneous sample. As a result digital audio systems can tolerate a larger number of residual errors, provided that they are detected, and thus concealment is possible. With a small number of exceptions computer storage does not need to operate in real time, either in record/write or playback/read. A reasonable extension of the time taken by either process is generally of no consequence. As a result computer recorders can perform functions such as read after write and retries. These processes can dramatically reduce the occurence of errors and so it becomes possible to upgrade the data integrity of a machine designed for audio recording primarily by attention to the way in which it is controlled.

As RDAT uses azimuth recording, the smallest physical unit of recording is the adjacent pair of tracks due to one head of each azimuth type crossing the tape. This track pair is called a frame and each frame is a self-contained error-correction structure. In DDS a fixed number of logical frames makes up a group, which is the smallest entity written to the tape. A group may have more physical frames than logical frames if a read-after-write check causes one or more frames to be rewritten. The variable size records from the host have to be mapped on to the fixed-size physical groups in a way which is transparent to the host.

A record is one entity which the host computer wants recorded. It can be a file mark, a save set mark or an arbitrary number of bytes of data.

Figure 5.25 shows that a group consists of 22 logical frames, or head pair passes, which are shared by host data and the DDS index information [9]. Each DDS frame is based on the data structure of RDAT and thus contains as many bytes as the RDAT frame contains audio sample bytes – 5760 bytes. In DDS, four bytes of this are used as a header, leaving 5756 bytes of data.

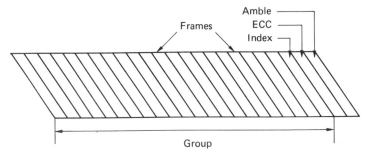

Figure 5.25

In 22 frames this results in a capacity of 126 632 bytes to be shared between host data and DDS group index. The group may be completed by an optional group error-correction frame which contains redundancy calculated on every frame in the group. Following this may be zero or more so-called amble frames. These do not store host data, but are considered to be part of the group they follow for access control purposes. The existence of groups is invisible to the host so that the system acts like a variable length record device. The DDS system will accept records of any length from the host and break them up to fit into the group structure. If the host sends short records several records may be stored in one group. If the host sends long records several groups will be needed to store one record. In this way maximum use is made of the physical storage space.

The way in which the records are mapped onto the group structure is stored in the group index, which is stored at the end of the group in the last data frame and grows towards the front according to the number of entries. File marks and save set marks are treated logically as records but they exist in the index only; they do not unnecessarily take up space in the data area.

As a number of filemarks and save set marks can exist anywhere within a group, the repeating subcode for each group contains file mark and save set mark counts which denote the number of marks recorded up to the end of that group. If more than one filemark (or save set mark) occurs in a group, the subcode filemark (or save set mark) count will be non-contiguous. If a DDS system is locating a file under host control it may be told to skip one or more save set marks. The transport will shuttle forwards at high speed, with the heads crossing tracks. By the end of a group the repeating subcode will have made it possible to read the filemark and save set mark counts despite the random head/track registration. If the mark count has exceeded the count which the system was looking for, the wanted mark must be within the current group. The DDS logic will read the group into a buffer and examine the index. The group index will then reveal the position in the buffer of the first record after the mark. The system can then assert ready to the host and if the host responds with a read command the record can be transmitted from the buffer. If the record runs over into the next group this fact will also be contained within the group index so the system will continue to fetch groups from tape until an end of record mark is found in the index.

The existing frame based error-correction strategy of RDAT is incorporated in DDS so that the LSI chips developed for the purpose can be used. As was shown in the section on RDAT C1,C2 error correction, this can correct a defect stretching over 2.5 mm length of track and so the normal RDAT error correction will only fail if this limit is exceeded. The C1 and C2 codes of RDAT were designed to correct a combination of uncorrelated random and burst errors. A large number of random errors will reduce the ability of the system to correct bursts. The 8/10 channel code of RDAT shows a slight pattern sensitivity in that not all of the channel bit groups are DC free and some of them are asymmetric, resulting in peak shift. On normal audio material the complexity of sound waveforms means that successive bytes seldom show any correlation and so the pattern sensitivity is randomized out. However, in computer data it is possible to encounter lists, tables and arrays where the same byte may be repeated. In some cases this will select one of the less optimal channel patterns regularly, and the increase in peak shift will reduce the immunity of the system to noise. In DDS the same channel coding as RDAT is used but the data are subjected to a randomizing process before recording. The signal recorded is the exclusive–OR function of the data and a pseudo-random sequence. This serves to decorrelate adjacent symbols and restores the error rate to that of the audio version. On replay the same pseudo-random sequence must be generated in synchronism with the symbols off tape in order to recreate the original data. Randomizing is always used in DDS; the remaining strategies are optional.

All error correction systems distort the relationship between raw or off-tape error rate and output or residual error rate. At low raw error rates the residual error rate is less. However, at some point, the performance of the error-correction system is exceeded and the graph bends, entering a region where the residual errors can become greater than the raw errors. Clearly, the system must be prevented from entering this region.

In RDAT the main reason for errors exceeding the capacity of the existing C1,C2 system is infrequent media defects [10]. Measurements on actual media show that defects tend to be roughly circular so that if a defect is large enough to exceed the error-correction power of one frame, then it will probably affect a large number of adjacent frames so that an additional C3 error-correcting code working across frames would be unable to correct it. A defect of this magnitude will, however, be easily detected by read-after-write. In this case the failing frame can be recorded elsewhere until it is successfully written. The system must be able to handle groups in which the number of physical or absolute frames exceeds the logical frame count of 22. Owing to the physical spacing between write and read heads, and the finite delay in deinterleaving data for error checking, a defective frame will not necessarily be identified until several more have been written. In this case, it is possible to repeat the faulty frame and all the frames which were recorded before it was decided to repeat, up to a maximum of five frames. Although this appears to be wasteful of tape, in fact it is not, because the presence of a defect large enough to cause a read-after-write failure will probably extend over several frames.

The repeated recordings are handled by an addressing system. The header at the beginning of the data area of each frame contains a logical frame number and these will correctly denote the frame number even if some frames are repeated. The system will simply use any copy of a frame which is not uncorrectable until it has identified enough different logical frames to assemble the group. One way in which this can be done is for the system to read ahead by up to six frames after an uncorrectable frame is found to see if it repeats, and then to resume reading.

In N-group writing, each group is written contiguously several times, up to a maximum of eight. The repeated groups are identical except for the absolute frame count and group count values. There is a two-bit repeat flag in the subcode, where one bit set denotes that a previous group is identical to this one, the other bit set denotes that the next group is identical. Clearly, N-group writing decreases tape capacity in proportion to N, but provides protection against gross events which can be expected in uncontrolled environments, and against certain transport defects.

A third option for increasing data integrity is the use of additional redundancy. Following the 44 data/index tracks in a group, an additional frame is recorded which produces codewords across the tracks. Every byte in a given position in each track is used to calculate the Reed–Solomon redundancy bytes in the same position in the C3 frame. If one or two tracks become uncorrectable by the usual C1,C2 correction within the frame, then this fact can be used as a pointer to correct that track by erasure. Only two tracks can be corrected in this fashion, however, and so protection against helical scratches, but not against two-dimensional defects, is provided.

Since there are three error-protection strategies, which are optional in any combination, there are eight ways in which a tape might be recorded. In fact the recording strategy may change along the length of the tape. A DDS system is only considered to comply with the standard if it can read all combinations, although it is only necessary to be able to record one of the combinations to be considered standard.

The most powerful DDS strategy is clearly read-after-write, since this effectively removes media defects as a source of error. It does, however, require a special RDAT transport, having additional heads mounted in the drum which read the data at least 270° after it is written. It is not necessary to perform a full decode to establish that a write error has occurred; a physical defect will result in a reduction in RF level. Checking of the inner codewords will reveal dropins due to contaminants between the record head and the tape.

The other optional strategies are available to drives which have only two heads and so cannot perform read-after-write.

5.7 The Compact Disc

The CD channel code has to operate under a number of constraints. These are

1. .The DC content of the code should be as small as possible for several reasons. Disc runout and contamination cause low frequency noise in the replay signal, which can be rejected if there is no information at these frequencies. Code DC content will also appear as noise in the tracking, and to a lesser extent the focus servos. Finally a DC-free code simplifies the design of the data separator.

2. .The efficiency of the code, which is the relationship of bit rate to channel bandwidth, should be high since this has a major influence on the playing time. Fortunately the jitter of a non-contact rigid medium is relatively low, which gives more freedom in the choice of coding scheme.

3. .The CD system depends heavily on the error-correction system, and a group code using symbols of the same size as the error-correction mechanism will be at an advantage because error propagation can be minimized.

4. .The bit rate of CD is low compared to that of computer disks and digital video recorders; thus no simplification of the code is required to achieve the necessary operating speed. A complex encoding system is a relatively small penalty because few encoders are needed. The complexity of the decoder is of greater significance since this more directly affects the cost of the player.

It was shown in Chapter 2 that there is a cut-off frequency due to the numerical aperture of the optics and the track velocity. All recorded frequencies must be below this by a sensible margin to allow a noise margin in the presence of coma due to disc warps and focus errors. This determines the minimum time period between transitions. It is fundamental to the CD channel code that the time between successive transitions (bump edges) is an integer multiple of one-third the minimum period. The basic time period T is one cycle of 4.3218 MHz or 231.4 ns. Figure 5.26 shows that the minimum wavelength allowable is $6T$ and that this corresponds to 720 kHz. The minimum period between transitions is $3T$, but the period can also be $4T$, $5T$, etc. In order to retain a reasonable clock content for immunity to jitter the

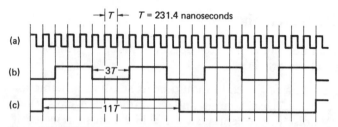

Figure 5.26 The limit frequencies of CD channel code: (a) the master clock frequency of 4.3218 MKz, T=231.4 ns; (b) the highest recorded frequency with transitions 3 T apart, frequency 720 kHz; (c) the lowest recorded frequency with transitions 11 T apart, frequency 196 kHz

maximum period between transitions (the run-length limit) is $11T$, corresponding to a frequency of 196 kHz. There are thus only nine different time periods used in all CD recording. The basic clock period is one-third the minimum transition length and so the resolution of the medium has apparently been increased by a factor of three. This gain cannot be fully realized because some data patterns cannot be recorded if the $3T$ spacing rule is to be obeyed. Data to be recorded must be converted to a form which accepts this restriction.

Symbols of $14T$ period are assembled. If all combinations of a 14-bit symbol are examined it will be found that there are some 267 where the run length is neither less than $3T$ nor more than $11T$. From these, 256 patterns are selected to describe uniquely any combination of eight data bits. Some of the remaining valid patterns are used for synchronizing.) Figure 5.27 shows some valid and invalid symbols for comparison. This conversion process gave rise to the name of eight-to-fourteen modulation (EFM) for the CD channel code.(To prevent violation of the rules by certain symbols following others, and to control the DC content of the code, three packing bits are placed between each symbol. Each eight-bit data symbol thus requires $17T$ to be recorded.) This coding is 8/17 efficient and when multiplied by the resolution improvement of three, yields the actual density ratio of EFM:

$$\frac{3 \times 8}{17} \times 100\% = 141\%$$

Although the highest frequency in the channel code is 720 kHz, or 1.44 million transitions per second, the bit rate is given by

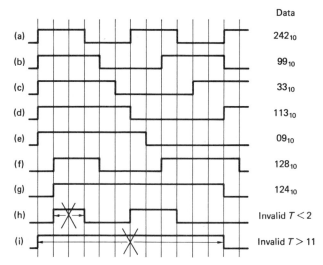

Figure 5.27 (a–g) Part of the codebook for EFM code showing examples of various run lengths from $3T$ to $11T$. (h, i) Invalid patterns which violate the run-length limits

$$4.3218 \times \frac{8}{17} \text{ Mbits/s} = 2 \text{ Mbits/s}$$

The choice of packing bits for DC control is determined as follows.

The digital sum value (DSV) of the channel patterns is derived as in Figure 5.28. If a channel bit is true during a T period, one is added to the DSV. If it is false, one is subtracted. Clearly, if the channel code is to be DC-free the DSV must average to zero. In Figure 5.28(b) two successive $14T$ symbols are shown, each of which has positive DSV. By adding a transition in the packing bits, the second symbol is inverted and the overall DSV is reduced. This inversion has no effect on the data as the only parameter of interest is the period between transitions.

The interference-readout process causes reflected light to increase and decrease about some average, which superimposes a DC level on the readout signal, in addition to a component at the rotation frequency of the disc and its harmonics. Since the code is DC-free a simple coupling capacitor can be used to remove these effects.

182

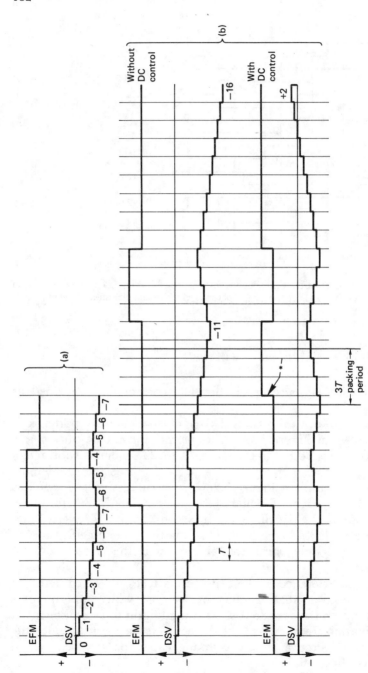

Figure 5.28 (a) Digital sum value example calculated from EFM waveform. (b) Two successive 14T symbols without DC control (upper) give DSV of −16. Additional transition (*) results in DSV of +2, anticipating negative content of next symbol

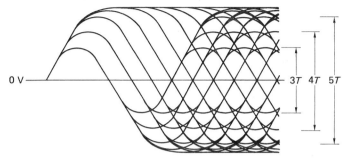

0 V — 3T 4T 5T

Figure 5.29 The characteristic eye pattern of EFM observed by oscilloscope. Note the reduction in amplitude of the higher frequency components. The only information of interest is the time when the signal crosses zero

If a typical readout signal is observed on an oscilloscope which triggers on a positive zero crossing, the next zero crossing could be $3T$, $4T$, etc., later as shown in Figure 5.29. The oscilloscope superimposes all these waveforms to give the characteristic eye pattern of CD. The $3T$ minimum and the $1T$ increments can be seen. Note that the amplitude of the shorter-period signals is smaller because of the linear fall in response to the cutoff frequency.

The quality of the optics and the focus servo can be assessed by comparing the $3T$ amplitude with maximum amplitude.

The first step in data separation is to locate the crossings in the signal and produce a binary waveform. This is done by comparing the input waveform with a reference voltage, a process referred to as slicing. Since the code is DC-free, the reference voltage, or slicing level, can be obtained by integrating the binary output (Figure 5.30). This recreates the binary channel code. Every readout transition is used to synchronize a phase-locked loop running with period T. This clock is used to count the number of T periods between transitions and thus recreate the $14T$ symbols. These are converted back to data bytes using a ROM or gate array. The truth table of the EFM conversion is computer-optimized to minimize the complexity of the decoder.

As with most channel codes EFM requires a preamble to synchronize the read circuitry to the $14T$ symbol boundaries. This unique preamble consists of three transitions seperated by $11T$.

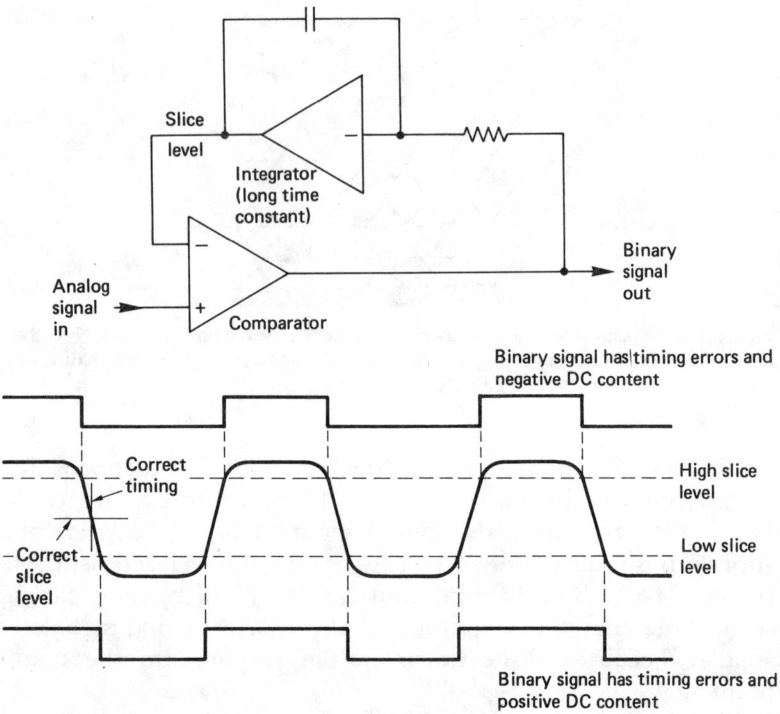

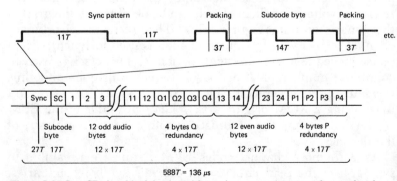

Figure 5.30 Self-slicing a DC-free channel code. Since the channel code signal from the disc is band-limited, it has finite rise times, and slicing at the wrong level (as shown here) results in timing errors, which cause the data separator to be less reliable. As the channel code is DC-free, the binary signal when correctly sliced should integrate to zero. An incorrect slice level gives the binary output a DC content and, as shown here, this can be fed back to modify the slice level automatically

Figure 5.31 One CD data block begins with a unique sync pattern, and one subcode byte, followed by 24 audio bytes and eight redundancy bytes. Note that each byte requires $14T$ in EFM, with $3T$ packing between symbols, making $17T$

Each data block or frame, shown in Figure 5.31 consists of 33 symbols $17T$ each following the preamble, making a total of $588T$ or $136\,\mu\text{s}$. Each symbol represents eight data bits. The first symbol in the block is used for subcode and the remaining 32 bytes represent 24 audio sample bytes and eight bytes of redundancy for the error-correction system. The subcode byte forms part of a subcode block which is built up over 98 successive data frames.

Figure 5.32 reveals the timing relationships of the CD format. The sampling rate of 44.1 kHz with 16-bit words in left and right channels results in an audio data rate of 176.4 kb/s (k = 1000 here, not 1024). Since there are 24 audio bytes in a data frame the frame rate will be

$$\frac{176.4}{24}\,\text{kHz} = 7.35\,\text{kHz}.$$

If this frame rate is divided by 98, the number of frames in a subcode block, the subcode block rate of 75 Hz results. This frequency can be divided down to provide a running-time display in the player.

If the frame rate is multiplied by 588, the number of channel bits in a frame, the master clock-rate of 4.3218 MHz results. Fom this the maximum and minimum frequencies in the channel, 720 kHz and 196 kHz, can be obtained using the run length limits of EFM.

5.8 CD frame contents

Each data frame contains 24 audio bytes but they are non-contiguous. The sequence of the audio bytes and their relationship to the redundancy bytes will now be discussed.

The error-correction system has to deal with a combination of large burst errors and random errors, and interleaving is used extensively to reduce the amount of redundancy necessary [11,12].

There are a number of interleaves used in CD, each of which has a specific purpose. The full interleave structure is shown in Figure 5.33. The first stage of interleave is to introduce a delay between odd and even samples. The effect is that uncorrectable errors cause odd samples and even samples to be destroyed at

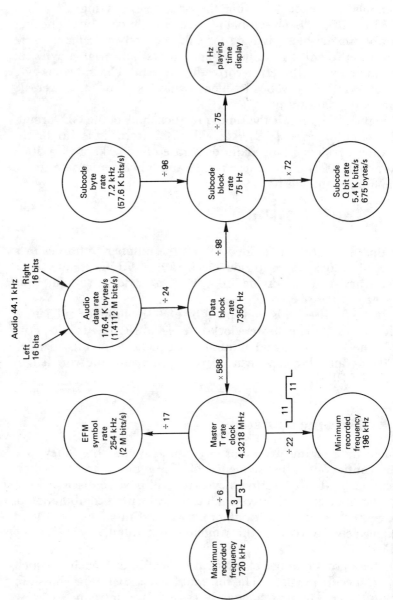

Figure 5.32 CD timing structure

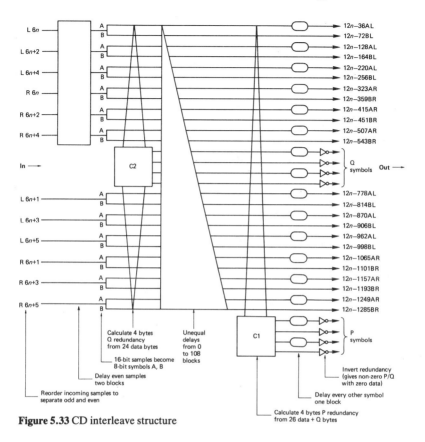

Figure 5.33 CD interleave structure

different times so that interpolation can be used to conceal the errors, with a reduction in audio bandwidth and a risk of aliasing. The odd/even interleave is performed first in the encoder since concealment is the last function in the decoder. Figure 5.34 shows that an odd/even delay of two blocks permits interpolation in the case where two uncorrectable blocks leave the error-correction system.

Left and right samples from the same instant form a sample set. As the samples are 16 bits, each sample set consists of four bytes, AL, BL, AR, and BR. Six sample sets form a 24-byte parallel word and the C2 encoder produces four bytes of redundancy Q. By placing the Q symbols in the centre of the block the odd/even distance is increased, permitting interpolation over the largest possible error burst. The 28 bytes are now

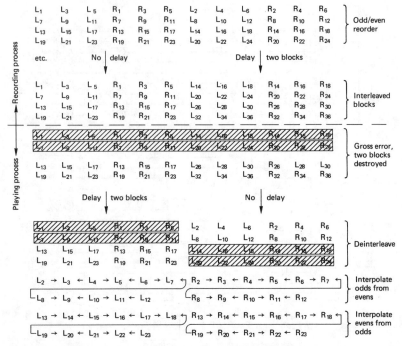

Figure 5.34 Odd/even interleave permits the use of interpolation to conceal uncorrectable errors

subjected to differing delays, which are integer multiples of four blocks. This produces a convolutional interleave where one C2 codeword is stored in 28 different blocks spread over a distance of 109 blocks.

At one instant, the C2 encoder will be presented with 28 bytes which have come from 28 different codewords. The C1 encoder produces a further four bytes of redundancy P. Thus the C1 and C2 codewords are produced by crossing an array in two directions. This is an example of crossinterleaving.

The final interleave is an odd/even output symbol delay, which causes P codewords to be spread over two blocks on the disc as shown in Figure 5.35. This mechanism prevents small random errors destroying more than one symbol in a P codeword. The choice of eight-bit symbols in EFM assists this strategy. The expressions in Figure 5.33 determine how the interleave is calculated. Figure 5.36 shows an example of the use

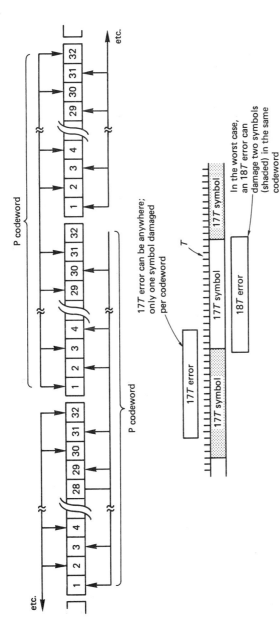

Figure 5.35 The final interleave of the CD format spreads P codewords over two blocks. Thus any small random error can only destroy one symbol in one codeword, even if two adjacent symbols in one block are destroyed. Since the P code is optimized for single-symbol error correction, random errors will always be corrected by the C1 proces, maximizing the burst-correcting power of the C2 process after deinterleave

190

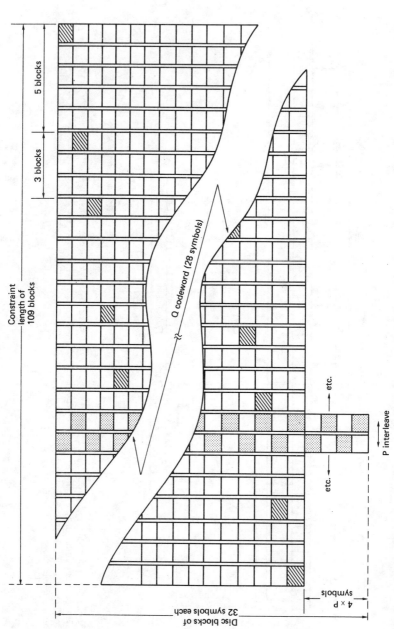

Figure 5.36 Owing to crossinterleave, the 28 symbols from the Q encode process (C2) are spread over 109 blocks, shown hatched. The final interleave of P code words (as in Figure 5.35) is shown stippled. Result of the latter is that Q code word has 5, 3, 5, 3 spacing rather than 4, 4

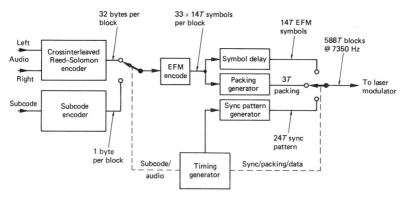

Figure 5.37 CD encoder which modulates cutting laser. Audio samples are crossinterleaved and combined with subcode data. These eight-bit symbols are encoded into 14 *T* EFM symbols. The packing generator prevents run-length violations and provides DC content control via 3 *T* packing symbols. The EFM symbol delay allows the packing generator to look ahead. Two of the many functions of the timing generator are to switch in subcode bytes (left) and to assemble blocks by selecting sync patterns, data and packing (right)

of these expressions to calculate the contents of a block and to demonstrate the crossinterleave.

The calculation of the P and Q redundancy symbols is made using Reed–Solomon cyclic polynomial division. The P redundancy symbols are primarily for detecting errors, to act as pointers or error flags for the Q system. The P system can, however, correct single-symbol errors.

Figure 5.37 shows a block diagram of a CD encoder which is used to drive the acousto-optic modulator in the cutter. Audio and subcode data streams are supplied and the crossinterleaved block structure is created. The EFM encoder produces a 14-channel-bit pattern for every eight-bit symbol, and sync patterns and merging bits are multiplexed in.

5.9 CD player structure

One of the design constraints of the Compact Disc and its format was that since they were to be mass produced, it should allow the construction of players to be straightforward.

Figure 5.38 shows the block diagram of a typical player and illustrates the essential components. The most natural division

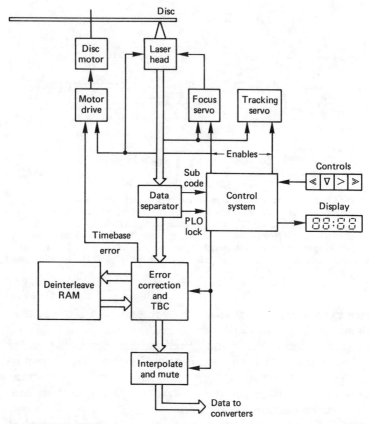

Figure 5.38 Block diagram of CD player showing the data path (broad arrow) and control servo systems

within the block diagram is into the control/servo system and the data path. The control system provides the interface between the user and the servo mechanisms and performs the logical interlocking required for safety and the correct sequence of operation.

The servo systems include the spindle-drive servo, and the focus and tracking servos. The data path consists of the data separator, timebase correction and the deinterleaving and error-correction process followed by the error-concealment mechanism. This results in a sample stream which is fed to the converters.

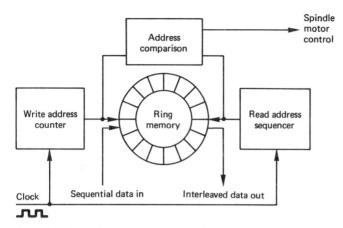

Figure 5.39 Deinterleaving is achieved by the use of a ring memory which is addressed linearly on one side and by a sequencer at the other side. Time base correction may also be performed by the same unit, and the relationship of read and write addresses can be used to control the disc spindle

The data separator converts the readout waveform into subcode bytes, audio samples, redundancy and a clock. The data stream and the clock will contain speed variations due to disc runout and chucking tolerances, and these have to be removed by a timebase corrector.

The timebase corrector is a memory addressed by counters which are arranged to overflow, giving the memory a ring structure, as shown in Figure 5.39. Writing into the memory is done using clocks from the data separator whose frequency rises and falls with runout, whereas reading is done using a crystal-controlled clock, which removes speed variations from the samples, and makes wow and flutter unmeasurable. The timebase-corrector will only function properly if the two addresses are kept apart. This implies that the long-term data rate from the disc must equal the crystal-clock rate. The disc speed can be controlled by analysing the address relationship of the timebase corrector. If the disc is turning too quickly the write address will move towards the read address; if the disc is turning too slowly the write address moves away from the read address. Subtraction of the two addresses produces an error signal which can be fed to the motor.

As the disc cutter produces constant bit density along the

track by reducing the rate of rotation as the track radius increases, the player will automatically duplicate that speed reduction. The actual linear velocity of the track will be the same as the velocity of the cutter, and although this will be constant for a given disc it can vary between 1.2 and 1.4 m/s on different discs.

Following data separation and timebase correction, the error-correction and deinterleave processes take place.

Because of the crossinterleave system there are two opportunities for correction, firstly using the C1 redundancy prior to deinterleaving, and secondly using the C2 redundancy after deinterleaving.

In Chapter 4 it was shown that interleaving is designed to spread the effects of burst errors among many different codewords so that the errors in each are reduced. However, the process can be impaired if a small random error, due perhaps to an imperfection in manufacture, occurs close to a burst error caused by surface contamination.

The function of the C1 redundancy is to correct single-symbol errors [13], so that the power of interleaving to handle bursts is undiminished, and to generate error flags for the C2 system when a gross error is encountered.

The EFM coding is a group code which means that a small defect which changes one channel pattern into another will have corrupted up to eight data bits. In the worst case if the small defect is on the boundary between two channel patterns two successive bytes could be corrupted. However, the final odd/even interleave on encoding ensures that the two bytes damaged will be in different C1 codewords; thus a random error can never corrupt two bytes in one C1 codeword, and random errors are therefore always correctable by C1. From this it follows that the maximum size of a defect considered random is $17T$ or $3.9\,\mu s$. This corresponds to about a $5\,\mu m$ length of the track. Errors of greater size are, by definition, burst errors.

The deinterleave process is achieved by writing sequentially into a memory and reading out using a sequencer. The RAM can perform the function of the timebase-corrector as well. The size of memory necessary follows from the format; the amount of interleave used is a compromise between the resistance to burst errors and the cost of the deinterleave memory. The maximum delay is 108 blocks of 28 bytes, and the minimum delay is negligible. It follows that a memory capacity of $54 \times 28 = 1512$ bytes is necessary.

Allowing a little extra for timebase error, odd/even interleave and error flags transmitted from C1 to C2, the convenient capacity of 2048 bytes is reached.

The C2 decoder is designed to locate and correct a single-symbol error or to correct two symbols whose locations are known. The former case occurs very infrequently as it implies that the C1 decoder has miscorrected. However, the C1 decoder works before deinterleave and there is no control over the burst-error size that it sees. There is a small but finite probability that random data in a large burst could produce the same syndrome as a single error in good data. This would cause C1 to miscorrect and no error flag would accompany the miscorrected symbols. Following deinterleave the C2 decode could detect and correct the miscorrected symbols as they would now be single-symbol errors in many codewords. The overall miscorrection probability of the system is thus quite minute. Where C1 detects burst errors, error flags will be attached to all symbols in the failing C1 codeword. After deinterleave in the memory these flags will be used by the C2 decoder to correct up to two corrupt symbols in one C2 codeword. Should more than two flags appear in one C2 codeword, the errors are uncorrectable, C2 flags the entire codeword bad, and the interpolator will have to be used. The final odd/even sample deinterleave makes interpolation possible because it displaces the odd corrupt samples relative to the even corrupt samples.

If the rate of bad C2 codewords is excessive the correction system is being overwhelmed and the output must be muted to prevent unpleasant noise. Unfortunately digital audio cannot be muted by simply switching the sample stream to zero because this would produce a click. It is necessary to fade down to the mute condition gradually by multiplying sample values by descending coefficients, usually in the form of a half-cycle of a cosine wave. This gradual fadeout requires some advance warning in order to be able to fade out before the errors arrive. This is achieved by feeding the fader through a delay. The mute status bypasses the delay and allows the fadeout to begin sufficiently in advance of the error. The final output samples of this system will be either correct, interpolated or muted, and these can then be sent to the convertors in the player.

5.10 CDROM

The Compact Disc's main advantage in a data storage application is its capacity in relation to cost. Since digital audio requires about one megabit per second per audio channel, one CD holds over 600 M bytes of audio data. This is the equivalent of about five reels of ½ inch computer tape, or some 200 000 pages of text. A CD player costs about the same as a floppy disc drive but holds three orders of magnitude more data.

Publishing houses are exploiting CDROM to store technical databases for commercial, financial and medical use. Several years' issues of all the major journals in a given discipline can be carried on a single disk, making optical disk publishing a reality. For business users the cost of a suitable computer and CDROM drive is trivial, and the cost of the disks is reasonable considering the storage space released. For the consumer, encyclopaedias will be the first application.

For cost reasons, CDROM players will rely on components designed for audio use and so access time will not be as good as hard disk drives, although it is comparable to the access time of floppy disks.

Unlike magnetic disks, CD uses a continuous spiral, so there is no equivalent of a cylinder address. Data on CDROM are addressed as a function of time along the track.

While interpolation to conceal uncorrectable errors is acceptable in digital audio it cannot be used in computer code. The residual error rate of CD must be reduced for data applications. In CDROM this is achieved by adding an extra layer of error correction on top of the existing CD format.

The sync block structure of CD was shown in Figure 5.31. This is maintained in CDROM so that the same mastering and playback equipment can be used. The basic unit of addressing in CD is the subcode block, which contains 98 sync blocks; CDROM maintains this structure, and the subcode block of CD becomes the CDROM codeword block for the additional error correction.

One subcode block contains $98 \times 24 = 2352$ bytes. The structure of this block in CDROM is shown in Figure 5.40, in a way which relates to the original application where stereo samples of 16-bit wordlength were conveyed. At the beginning is a sync field, which is all ones except for the first and last bytes

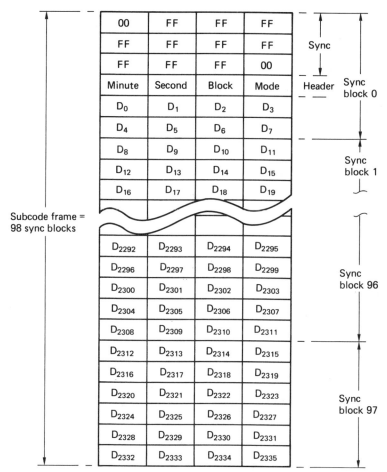

00	FF	FF	FF
FF	FF	FF	FF
FF	FF	FF	00
Minute	Second	Block	Mode
D_0	D_1	D_2	D_3
D_4	D_5	D_6	D_7
D_8	D_9	D_{10}	D_{11}
D_{12}	D_{13}	D_{14}	D_{15}
D_{16}	D_{17}	D_{18}	D_{19}
D_{2292}	D_{2293}	D_{2294}	D_{2295}
D_{2296}	D_{2297}	D_{2298}	D_{2299}
D_{2300}	D_{2301}	D_{2302}	D_{2303}
D_{2304}	D_{2305}	D_{2306}	D_{2307}
D_{2308}	D_{2309}	D_{2310}	D_{2311}
D_{2312}	D_{2313}	D_{2314}	D_{2315}
D_{2316}	D_{2317}	D_{2318}	D_{2319}
D_{2320}	D_{2321}	D_{2322}	D_{2323}
D_{2324}	D_{2325}	D_{2326}	D_{2327}
D_{2328}	D_{2329}	D_{2330}	D_{2331}
D_{2332}	D_{2333}	D_{2334}	D_{2335}

Sync / Header — Sync block 0

Sync block 1

Subcode frame = 98 sync blocks

Sync block 96

Sync block 97

Figure 5.40 Arrangement of CD-rom data corresponding to 98 sync blocks, or one subcode block. There is a 12-byte sync pattern and a four-byte header, leaving 2320 bytes for user data and redundancy

which are zeros. The next four bytes specify the time along the track from the beginning in minutes, seconds and subcode blocks (1–75), and the mode. This track timing is the same as will be carried in the Q subcode, but it is repeated in the data field so that CDROM players do not need to communicate subcode to the host computer.

198

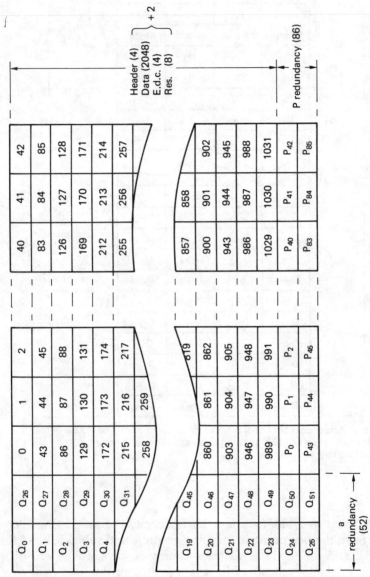

Figure 5.41 (a) The additional error correction of CD-rom. The P redundancy is formed on columns of the array, whereas Q redundancy is diagonal, as shown at b

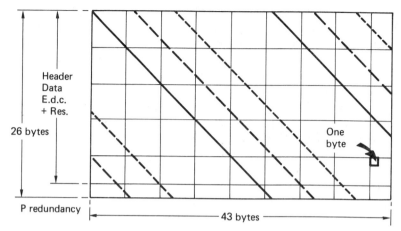

Figure 5.41 (b) in the block-completed cross interleave of CD-rom's additional error correction, diagonal Q code words wrap around so that 26 of them cover all of the block's contents

Following the header are 2336 bytes, made up of 2048 bytes of user data, 8 bytes reserved for future use and 280 bytes of redundancy.

The capacity of CDROM can now be calculated. Although CD can play for up to 75 minutes, this reduces the track linear speed and raises the raw error rate. CDROM is restricted to 1 hour, resulting in longer minimum wavelengths on the data track. Since the subcode block rate is 75 Hz it is easy to obtain the user data rate of $75 \times 2\,K = 150\,Kbytes$ per second. The overall capacity can be found by multiplying this figure by the playing time in seconds: $60 \times 60 \times 150\,Kbytes = 540\,Mbytes$

The additional error correction needed by CDROM also uses Reed–Solomon coding over GF(256), which means that the symbols are byte sized. Figure 5.41(a) shows how the data corresponding to one subcode period are arranged: 16-bit words are split into high byte and low byte and formed into two identical arrays. Each one is 43 columns wide. The first 24 rows contain the four-byte header, the 2 Kbytes of user data, and a four-byte CRCC calculated over the header and data. Each column of the array is then made into a P codeword by the addition of two bytes of Reed–Solomon redundancy, which occupies another two rows in the array. To give a crossinterleaved structure, Q codewords are then generated on diagonals throughout the array. Figure 5.41(b) shows how these diagonals wrap around to form what is known as a block completed cross-interleave. The two bytes of Q redundancy for each diagonal is contained in two additional columns added to the left of the array.

When a CDROM is played, the existing CD player chip set will be able to perform up to four corrections by erasure on each outer codeword. If this is exceeded by raw errors, the chip set will generate uncorrectable error flags so that concealment can be used in an audio player. These flags can also be used as erasure flags for the extra layer of error correction in CDROM, but this requires an extra connection which is not always implemented. Each of the additional codes can locate and correct single-byte errors but this could be doubled if player flags were available. The additional layer of error correction is often performed by software in the host computer to reduce hardware costs. Once correction has been performed, the CRC check is made and if this is satisfactory the data are assumed error-free.

5.11 Digital video recorders

The two digital VTR formats, now known as D-1 and D-2, are fundamentally different because they have each been optimized for a different application. The reasons behind the existence of two formats will be explained in terms of the systems in which they might be used, followed by a technical comparison of the coding systems.

Broadcasting standards must, by definition, last for an extremely long time since a change to an incompatible format would render obsolete a nation's entire installed base of receivers. Clearly, it would be impossible to produce new receivers for every household at once. Television broadcasting is thus continuously forced to make compromises between advances in technology and the need to broadcast to some agreed standard.

The introduction of colour to television was a technical advance but it was made more difficult because the broadcast colour picture had to be compatible with existing receivers.

The NTSC system added a subcarrier to the existing 525/60 monochrome standard. The spectrum of the subcarrier was designed to fit half-way between the sidebands of the luminance signal so that they could be separated by a colour receiver and would cancel on the screen of a monochrome set. Unfortunately the sound carrier had been set in such a spectral notch to prevent sound/picture interference, and there was now sound/chroma crosstalk. The sound carrier frequency could not be changed because existing sets would not then be able to tune to it. The solution was to move the spectrum of the video by slightly reducing the field rate. This 0.1% change was within the scan lock range of the receiver but it meant that the field rate was no longer simply related to real time. Drop frame timecode was invented to resolve the difference. The subcarrier frequency necessary to interleave sidebands meant that four fields would elapse before the same relationship existed between frame, line and subcarrier.

The PAL system was similarly based on the 625/50 monochrome system with the addition of a subcarrier. The main difference with PAL is that the alternating line principle split the chroma spectrum such that chroma energy was positioned at one-quarter and three-quarters of the space between luminance sidebands. This neatly avoided the sound/chroma crosstalk, but meant that the subcarrier frequency was such that eight fields would elapse before the same frame, line and subcarrier relationship repeated.

The introduction of colour to broadcasting meant new cameras, which had three tubes, red green and blue, and produced from them three simultaneous pictures on three separate wires. This was most inconvenient for installations which had previously distributed monochrome video which only needed a single signal. As the signal would ultimately become a single composite waveform with a subcarrier for broadcast, it was argued that the sooner the signal was encoded from RGB to composite, the easier it would be to distribute. The design of the video recorder could be adapted to accommodate the subcarrier without fundamental change, since only one recording channel was necessary with a composite signal. The typical video installation thus encoded at the camera and all subsequent operations, including recording, were carried out on the composite waveform.

The monochrome signal was relatively simple to edit since it was only necessary to follow an odd field with an even field at all times for a satisfactory result. The addition of the subcarrier meant that extra care had to be taken at edit points so that the subcarrier was continuous. This meant in NTSC that the four-field sequence had to be maintained over an edit point, and in PAL the eight-field sequence had to be maintained. Failure to do this resulted in a two-field (NTSC) or four-field (PAL) edit, which would cause an inversion in the subcarrier over the edit point. In order to maintain subcarrier phase in the machine output the timebase corrector would physically shift the lines by a distance corresponding to half a cycle of subcarrier. To overcome these difficulties a colour framing flag was inserted in the control track of the recorder every four or eight fields; relationships were established between frame number in timecode and the colour framing sequence; and microprocessor controlled editors were developed which could perform colour framed edits automatically.

Unlike digital audio the advent of digital technology in video was not with the digital recorder. The sheer bit rate necessary was one difficulty, and the need to achieve a high packing density to compete with the tape consumption of analog machines was another. Apart from standards convertors, whose high cost could be justified by the great need for international interchange, the first digital video product was the timebase corrector for analog video recorders.

As the cost of semiconductors fell it became feasible to manipulate video digitally and special effects machines came into being which could zoom and rotate the picture.

One thing which all digital effects machines have in common is that they cannot use composite video directly; it must be decoded first. The reason is simply that if the length of a video line is changed by some manipulation, the frequency of the subcarrier will also change and the colour information will become meaningless. In a composite environment, effects machines need a decoder on the input and an encoder on the output, so that processing takes place on baseband luminance and colour difference signals. Where a complex multi-faceted effect is being created, it may be necessary to produce each facet of the picture on a different pass through the effects machine. The result is pieced together by keying a new piece of the picture into the previous generation recording. Clearly, the video recorder must be capable of many generations of recording without degradation but, more importantly, the image may have been subject to several successive encodings and decodings (codecs), each one of which introduces some degradation.

Issues such as this were considered when the lengthy process of standardization which led to the D-1 digital tape format began. It was decided from the outset that the machine would record luminance and colour difference signals so that a recording could be made direct from a suitable camera without an intervening subcarrier encoding stage. The recording could be replayed directly into a digital effects machine or digital mixer/keyer without decoding. The use of colour difference recording makes editing more flexible because the only framing necessary at an edit point is to maintain the odd/even field sequence. The CCIR 601 digital video interconnect standard was developed to allow digital colour difference machines from different manufactures to communicate.

The sampling rate of 13.5 MHz is compatible with both 525 and 625 line systems and is designed to be line synchronous so that samples on sequential lines form vertical columns. This is important for the kind of manipulations performed in effects machines. The colour difference signals have a reduced bandwidth requirement and the sampling rate can be reduced accordingly. In D-1 the colour difference signals are sampled at half the rate of luminance, thus for every four luminance samples there will be two samples from each colour difference signal. This led to the description of D-1 as a 4:2:2 system.

The effect of sampling in this way is to produce data at an instantaneous rate of 27 megabytes per second or 216 megabits per second. This rate cannot be used directly to compute the overall data rate since in digital machines the blanked portion of the video need not be stored, so the data rate falls somewhat. However, the need to add redundancy for the purposes of error correction virtually returns the overall bit rate to the above figure.

In view of the high bit rate, short wavelength recording would be essential, and this is more susceptible to tape contamination. This and other factors mandated the use of a cassette to protect the tape and ease the threading process. It was not possible to specify a single cassette which would simultaneously hold enough tape for the longest recording time envisaged and yet be small enough to allow portable machines or convenient handling of short program segments or commercials. As a result three cassette sizes have been standardized which offer playing times of 11, 34 and 76 minutes [16]. The spacing of the reel hubs differs between the cassette sizes and machines which accept more than one cassette size need to have movable hubs. The cassette design is extremely thorough and the tape is well protected when out of the machine since doors cover both sides of the exposed run between the spools. The reels are automatically locked against rotation when in storage.

Unfortunately the D-1 format has not found wide acceptance with broadcasters since it cannot be installed in the existing composite video environment because it is simply not cost effective to replace the entire signal chain with colour diference hardware to obtain the benefit of digital recording [17]. The format has been used when a digital post-production facility has been planned from the outset to use colour difference working exclusively.

When Ampex began to develop the replacement for the quadruplex based ACR-25 cartridge machine, which is used extensively for automated broadcasting commercials, it was decided that digital recording would be used to offer transparent picture quality. Study of the environment in which a broadcast cartridge machine operates showed that the most appropriate technique would be to digitize the composite waveform.

Figure 5.42 illustrates the thinking which led to the composite DVTR. At (a) is shown an analog C-format VTR, which replays through a digital timebase corrector. Here, the composite signal is digitized and subjected to a variable delay in a memory in order to synchronize the output video with station reference. At (b) the analog recorder has been bypassed and memory has been extended by incorporating a digital cassette tape deck. The result is a D-2 composite digital VTR. Clearly, there is only one conversion to and from the digital domain, exactly as in the TBC of the analog recorder, and so there will be no more signal degradation due to conversion than in the analog case. However, the use of digital recording means that moiré, tape noise and velocity errors are eliminated. Excepting gross defects, dropouts do not normally need to be concealed because the use of error correction allows the original sample values to be computed.

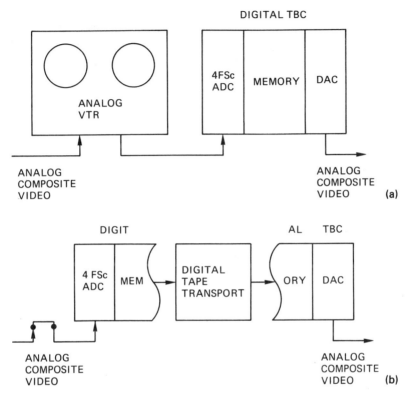

Figure 5.42 At (a) a conventional analog VTR is followed by a digital TBC which converts to and from the digital domain internally. At (b) the analog VTR is bypassed, and the TBC memory is extended by the use of a digital recorder. The number of conversions remains the same as in (a)

The strength of digital recording is that the recorder proper is transparent due to the use of error correction. The only degradation possible is due to the accuracy of conversion.

The sampling rate used in D-2 is four times the frequency of subcarrier (4FSc). This is higher than is necessary just to meet the criterion of sampling theory, but there are numerous important reasons for choosing this figure. When a composite video tape is played at other than normal speed, fields must be repeated or skipped in order to maintain the broadcast field rate. This necessarily destroys the continuity of the subcarrier which only repeats after four or eight fields in normal play. To produce a broadcastable picture, the out-of-sequence chroma must be decoded and re-encoded with the correct subcarrier phase. Using a sampling rate of 4FSc makes the process much simpler because if the sampling phase is carefully controlled with respect to the subcarrier the sampling process partially decodes the chroma. A digital filter to remove luminance information is easier to construct if the frequency to be rejected is related to the sampling frequency. A further advantage of the high sampling rate is that the antialiasing filter prior to the sampling stage need not have such a steep roll off from the passband edge to the Nyquist frequency, and so this filter can be more easily optimized for phase linearity and low passband ripple, which are important for multigeneration work.

These sampling rates work out at 14.32 MHz for NTSC and 17.72 MHz for PAL. Since composite recording only requires a single data channel, these figures also become the instantaneous byte rate, corresponding to 114 megabits per second and 141.76 megabits per second respectively.

As so much consideration had been given to the cassette intended for D-1, it made good sense to use the same cassette shell for the composite machine. As the composite digital format developed it became increasingly evident that broadcasters were not willing to make the huge investment necessary to convert their signal chains to colour difference working in order to use D-1 recorders. What the market needed was a machine which worked with composite signals, so that it could directly replace existing analog machines, but which offered the benefits of digital recording. There is a distinct analogy here with what has happened in professional digital audio, where digital multitrack recorders have found wide acceptance, but these are predominantly used in conjunction with existing analog mixing consoles. These digital multitracks are equipped with convertors so that they can interface to existing signals in a recording studio and form a plug-in replacement for analog recorders. The D-2 format came into being to fulfil this requirement. As with audio recorders, the digital composite machine has to be able to offer, at the least, every feature of the analog machines it is intended to replace, and be competitive in unit and running cost. This has been achieved; in fact the first generation of D-2 production recorders offers more features than C-format in addition to digital quality.

Although D-1 and D-2 share the same cassette shell they do not use the same tape and the method of recording is different: D-1 uses a conventional oxide coating on 16 micrometre thick tape, whereas D-2 uses metal particle tape which is 13 micrometres thick and which has higher coercivity. Since this produces more energy on playback, the tracks in D-2 at 35 μm are narrower than those of D-1 at 40 μm.

D-1 uses guard bands between the tracks to prevent crosstalk from one track to the next, and randomized NRZI channel code. In D-2, the Miller[2] channel code is used. This code is characterized by having a narrower spectrum, which is free of low frequencies irrespective of the data recorded, and so is ideal for use in conjunction with azimuth recording. The track pitch of D-2 is thus the same as the track width, whereas in D-1 the width of the guard band has to be added to the track width to give a pitch of 45 μm. The result of the combination of metal particle tape, azimuth recording and Miller[2] code allows much higher recording density than in D-1. Although the data rate of composite digital is a little less than the data rate of colour difference, the D-2 format achieves nearly three times the playing time of D-1 on the same size cassette, which allows greater operational flexibility and lower running cost.

Figure 5.43 contrasts the track layouts of the two formats. Both are segmented formats in that more than one diagonal track is needed to build up a television field. In D-1 the data rate is the same irrespective of whether the TV signals are 525/60 or 625/50. One segment on the tape consists of two tracks and the segment rate is 300 Hz. Six segments hold one field in the 50 Hz version and five segments hold one field in the 60 Hz version.

In D-2, the data rates differ so much between PAL and NTSC that a common scanner speed was not feasible. In D-2, the NTSC version uses six segments per field so that the segment rate is 360 Hz, whereas in PAL, eight segments per field are used, giving a segment rate of 400 Hz. The segment rates are different because the drum speeds are different. This does not, however, cause the tape speed or consumption to change. In PAL the drum speed rises but this results in narrower tracks.

The effect of the narrower tracks is that there is slightly less playback energy but this is offset by the fact that the higher head to tape speed raises the playback signal. In many respects D-2 is a high bit rate version of RDAT.

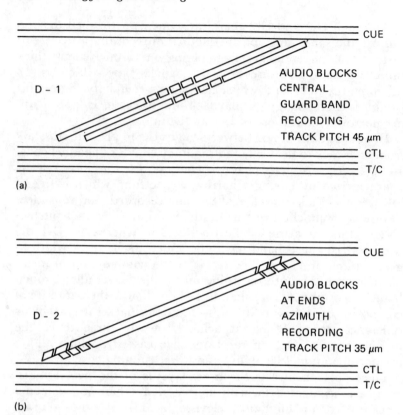

Figure 5.43 The track layouts of D-1 and D-2 are contrasted here. Note particularly the position of the audio blocks the use of azimuth recording in D-2

5.12 Audio in D-1 and D-2

The sensitivity of audio to error is greater than that of video, so in both formats the audio samples are recorded twice. The distribution of audio data is such that the second copy of the audio will be in a different position across the width of the tape, and be replayed with a different head. This gives immunity to longitudinal tape scratches and head clogs. In D-1 the audio samples are recorded centrally in the head sweep because tracking error is the least there. In D-2 the azimuth recording process is less sensitive to tracking error, allowing the audio blocks to be placed at the ends of the head sweeps. This has a number of advantages. When playing the tape at a speed substantially different from normal, the audio will not be needed. Placing the audio at the end of the head sweep allows the track-following heads longer to jump and settle. In a 180° wrap drum, one head pair writes one copy of the audio just before leaving the tape, when the other head pair contacts the tape to write the other copy. This minimizes the amount of memory needed for double recording. The central position of the audio blocks is a drawback of D-1 as it reduces the time available for heads to jump and limits the variable speed range.

5.13 Error correction in D-1 and D-2

The interleave and error correction systems will now be discussed. Figure 5.44 shows a conceptual block diagram of the system used in both formats which differ in detail rather than in principle.

Both D-1 and D-2 use a product code formed by producing Reed–Solomon codewords at right angles across an array. The array is formed in a memory and the layout used in D-2 can be seen in Figure 5.45. Incoming samples (bytes) are written into the array in columns. Each column is then made into a codeword by the addition of four bytes of redundancy, whereas D-1 has only two bytes. These are the outer codewords. Each row of the array is then formed into six inner codewords by the addition of eight bytes of redundancy to each. In order to make a recording, the memory is read in rows and two inner code words fit into one block along the track. Every block in an eight-field sequence is given a unique header address. This process continues until the entire array has been laid on tape to form a segment. The process then repeats for the other record head pair. In D-1 the process is similar except that the inner codewords only have four check bytes. Writing the memory in columns and reading in rows achieves the necessary interleave.

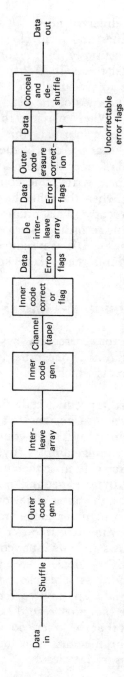

Figure 5.44 Block diagram of error correction strategy of DVTR. See text for details

211

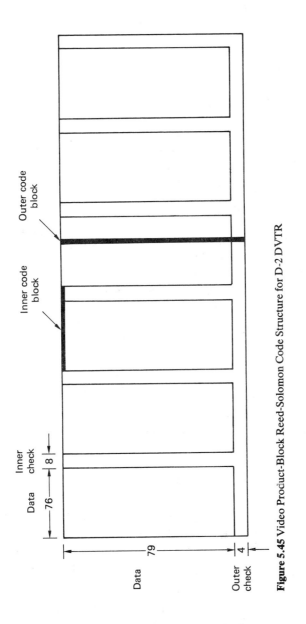

Figure 5.45 Video Product-Block Reed-Solomon Code Structure for D-2 DVTR

On replay, a combination of random errors and burst errors will occur. Data will come from tape in the sequence of the inner code words. In D-2 each of these has eight bytes of redundancy, so it would be possible to locate and correct up to four bytes in error in the code word. This, however, is not done because it is better to limit the correction power to three bytes and use the remaining redundancy to decrease the probability of miscorrection. In this way random errors are corrected with a high degree of confidence. Errors exceeding three bytes cause the entire inner codeword to be declared corrupt and it is written into the appropriate row of the deinterleave array as all zeros, with error flags set. D-1 is restricted to correcting up to two bytes. When all the rows of the array are completed it is possible to begin processing the columns. A burst error on tape which destroys one or more inner codewords will result in single-byte errors with flags in many different outer codewords. The presence of the error flags means that the outer code does not need to compute the position of the errors, so the full power of the outer code redundancy is available for correction. The four redundancy bytes of D-2 can correct four error bytes as compared with two bytes in D-1. The process of using error flags to assist a code is called erasure. It will be evident that enormous damage must be done to the tape track before four bytes are corrupted in a single outer codeword, which gives high resistance to dropouts and tape scratches. The error correction strategy of D-2 is more powerful than that of D-1, but this is as it should be since D-2 has a higher recording density. Table 5.2 compares the main error correction parameters of D-1 and D-2 [18].

5.14 Concealment and shuffle

In the event of a gross error, correction may not be possible, and some bytes may be declared uncorrectable. In this case the errors must be concealed by interpolation from adjacent samples. Due to the regular structure of the product code block uncorrectable burst errors would show up as a regular pattern of interpolations on the screen. The eye is extremely good at finding such patterns so the visibility is higher than might be expected. The solution to this problem is to perform a two-dimensional pseudo-random shuffle on the video samples

Table 5.2 Comparison of error correction coding system parameters[1]

Parameter	D-2	D-1
Inner block symbol size	8 *bits*	8 *bits*
Inner block size, data	76^2	60
Inner block size, check	8	4
Video outer block symbol size	8 *bits*	8 *bits*
Video outer block size, data	79	30
Video outer block size, check	4	2
Video product block interleave depth	6 *inner blocks*	10 *inner blocks*
Correctable video burst	≤ 2064	≤ 1340
Audio outer block symbol size	8 *bits*	4 *bits*
Audio outer block size, data	8	7 *nibbles*
Audio outer block size, check	4	3 *nibbles*
Audio product block interleave depth	1 *inner block*	1 *inner block*
Correctable audio burst[3]	≤ 344	≤ 198

Notes: 1. Table values in bytes unless otherwise indicated
2. Inner block size does not include identification pattern
3. Without utilizing duplication of audio data

before generating the product code. The reverse shuffle is performed on replay. The positions of interpolated samples due to an uncorrected error now form a pseudo-random pattern with much decreased visibility.

5.15 Defect handling in disks

The protection of data recorded on disks differs considerably from the approach used on other media, largely because the random access of disks allows possibilities denied to tape.

In the same way that magnetic tape is subject to dropouts, magnetic disks suffer from surface defects whose effect is to corrupt data. The shorter wavelengths employed as disk densities increase are affected more by a given size of defect. Attempting to make a perfect disk is subject to a law of diminishing returns and eventually a state is reached where it becomes more cost-effective to invest in a defect-handling system.

There are four main methods of handling media defects in magnetic media, and further techniques are needed in WORM laser disks, whose common goal is to make their presence transparent to the data. These methods vary in complexity and cost of implementation, and can often be combined in a particular system.

5.16 Bad-block files

In the construction of bad-block files, a brand new disk is tested by the operating system. Known patterns are written everywhere on the disk and these are read back and verified. Following this the system gives the disk a volume name and creates on it a directory structure which keeps records of the position and size of every file subsequently written. The physical disk address of every block which fails to verify is allocated to a file which has an entry in the disk directory. In this way, when genuine data files come to be written the bad blocks appear to the system to be in use storing a fictitious file, and no attempt will be made to write there. Some disks have dedicated tracks where defect information can be written during manufacture or by subsequent verification programs and these permit a speedy construction of the system bad-block file.

In association with the bad-block file, many drives allocate bits in each header to indicate that the associated block is bad. If a data transfer is attempted at such a block the presence of these bits causes the function to be aborted. The bad-block file system gives very reliable protection against defects but can result in a lot of disk space being wasted. Systems often use several disk blocks to store convenient units of data, called clusters, which will all be written or read together. Figure 5.46 shows how a bit map is searched to find free space and illustrates how the presence of one bad block can write off a whole cluster.

1	1	1	1	1	1	1	1	1	1	1	0	0	0	0	0	A
A	0	0	0	0	0	0	1	1	1	1	1	1	1	1	1	1
1	1	1	1	1	1	1	1	1	1	1	1	1	1	1	1	
1	1	1	1	1	1	1	0	0	0	0	1	0	0	0	0	B
0	0	1	1	1	1	1	1	1	1	1	1	1	0	0	0	
0	0	0	0	0	0	0	0	e	tc.							

Figure 5.46 A disk-block-usage bit map in 16-bit memory for a cluster size of 11 blocks. Before writing on the disk, the system searches the bit map for contiguous free space equal to or larger than the cluster size. The first available space is the second cluster shown at A above, but the next space is unusable because the presence of a bad block B destroys the contiguity of the cluster. Thus one bad block causes the loss of a cluster

5.17 Sector skipping

In sector skipping, space is made at the end of every track for a spare data block, which is not normally accessible to the system. Where a track is found to contain a defect the affected block becomes a skip sector. In this block the regular defect flags will be set but, in addition, a bit known as the skip-sector flag is set in this and every subsequent block in the track. When the skip-sector flag is encountered the effect is to add one to the desired sector address for the rest of the track, as shown in Figure 5.47. In this way the bad block is unused and the track format following the bad block is effectively slid along by one block to bring into use the spare block at the end of the track.

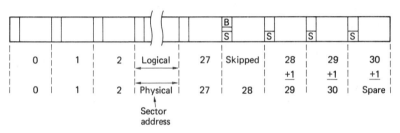

Figure 5.47 Skip sectoring. The bad block in this example has a physical sector address of 28. By setting the skip-sector flags in the header, this and subsequent logical blocks have one added to their sector addresses, and the spare block is brought into use

Using this approach the presence of single bad blocks does not cause the loss of clusters but requires slightly greater control complexity. If two bad blocks exist in a track the second will be added to the bad-block file as usual.

5.18 Defect skipping

The two techniques described so far have treated the block as the smallest element. In practice, the effect of a typical defect is to corrupt only a few bytes. The principle of defect skipping is that media defects can be skipped over within the block so that a block containing a defect is made usable. The header of each block contains the location of the first defect in bytes away from the end of the header, and the number of bytes from the first defect to the second defect, and so on up to the maximum of four

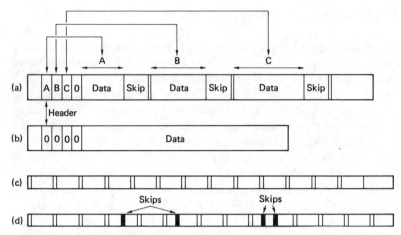

Figure 5.48 Defect skipping. (a) A block containing three defects. The header contains up to four parameters which specify how much data is to be written before each skip. In this example only three entries are needed. (b) An error-free block for comparison with (a); the presence of the skips lengthens in the block. To allow for this lengthening, the track contains spare space at the end, as shown in (c), which is an error-free track. (d) A track containing the maximum of four skips, which have caused the spare space to be used up

shown in the example of Figure 5.48. Each defect is overwritten with a fixed number of bytes of preamble code and a sync pattern. The skip is positioned so that there is sufficient undamaged preamble after the defect for the data separator to regain lock. Each defect lengthens the block, causing the format of the track to slip round. A space is left at the end of each track to allow a reasonable number of skips to be accommodated. Often a track descriptor is written at the beginning of each track which contains the physical position of defects relative to index. The disk format needed for a particular system can then be rapidly arrived at by reading the descriptor and translating the physical defect locations into locations relative to the chosen sector format. Figure 5.49 shows how a soft-sectoring drive can have two different formats around the same defects using this principle.

In the case where there are too many defects in a track for the skipping to handle, the system bad-block file will be used. This is rarely necessary in practice, and the disk appears to be contiguous error-free logical and physical space. Defect skipping

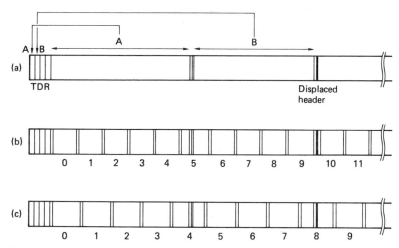

Figure 5.49 The purpose of the track descriptor record (TDR) is to keep a record of defects independent of disk format. The positions of the defects stored in the TDR (a) are used by the formatter to establish the positions relative to the format used. With the format (b), the first defect appears in sector 5, but the same defect would be in sector 4 for format (c). The second defect falls where a header would be written in (b) so the header is displaced for sector 10. The same defect falls in the data area of sector 8 in (c)

requires fast processing to deal with events in real time as the disk rotates. Bit-slice microsequencers are one approach because a typical microprocessor would be too slow.

5.19 Revectoring

A refinement of sector skipping which permits the handling of more than one bad block per track without the loss of a cluster is revectoring. A bad block caused by a surface defect may only have a few defective bytes so it is possible to record highly redundant information in the bad block. On a revectored disk a bad block will contain in the data area repeated records pointing to the address where data displaced by the defect can be found. The spare block at the end of the track will be the first such place and can be read within the same disk revolution, but out of sequence, which puts extra demands on the controller. In the less frequent case of more than one defect in a track, the second and subsequent bad blocks revector to spare blocks available in

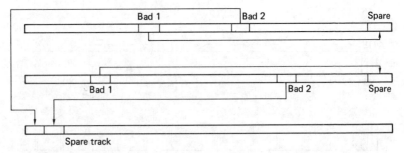

Figure 5.50 Revectoring. The first bad block in each track is revectored to the spare block at the end of the track. Unlike skip sectoring, subsequent good blocks are unaffected, and the replacement block is read out of sequence. The second bad block on any one track is revectored to one of a number of spare tracks kept on the disk for this purpose

an area dedicated to that purpose. The principle is illustrated in Figure 5.50. In this case a seek will be necessary to locate the replacement block. The low probability of this means that access time is not significantly affected.

5.20 Error correction in disks

The steps outlined above are the first line of defence against errors in disk drives and serve to ensure that, by and large, the errors due to obvious surface defects are eliminated. The absence of burst errors means that interleaving is not necessary, and this removes a potential cause of delay in data access. There are the remaining error mechanisms, such as noise and jitter, which can result in random errors, and it is necessary to protect disk data against these also. The error-correction mechanisms described in Chapter 4 will be employed. In general, each data block is made into a codeword by the addition of redundancy at the end. The error-correcting code used in disks was, for a long time, Fire code, because it allowed correction with the minimum circuit complexity. It could, however, only correct one error burst per block, and it had a probability of miscorrection which was marginal for some applications. The advances in complex logic chips meant that the adoption of a Reed–Solomon code was a logical step since these have the ability to correct multiple error bursts.

In some systems, the occurrence of errors is monitored to see if they are truly random or if an error persistently occurs in the same physical block. If this is the case, and the error is small and well within the correction power of the code, the block will continue in use. If, however, the error is larger than some threshold, the data will be read, corrected and rewritten elsewhere and the block will then be added to the bad-block file so that it will not be used again.

5.21 Defect handling in WORM disks

In erasable optical disks formatting is possible to map out defects in the same way as for magnetic disks, but in WORM disks it is not possible to verify the medium because it can only be written once. The presence of a defect cannot be detected until an attempt has been made to write on the disk. The data written can then be read back and checked for error. If there is an error in the verification, the block concerned will be rewritten, usually in the next block along the track. This verification process slows down the recording operation, but some drives have a complex optical system which allows a low-powered laser to read the track in between pulses of the writing laser, and can verify the recording as it is being made.

References

1. TANAKA, K., YAMAGUCHI, T. and SUGIYAMA, Y. (1979) Improved two-channel PCM tape recorder for professional use. Presented at 64th Audio Engineering Society Convention (New York, 1979), preprint 1533(G-3)
2. TANAKA, K., OZAKI, M., INOUE, T. and FURUKAWA, T. (1986) Application of generalized product code for stationary-head-type professional digital audio recorder. *Trans. IECE Japan*, **E 69**, 740–749
3. ISHIDA, Y. *et. al.* (1986) A professional use 2-channel digital audio recorder adopting an improved signal format. Presented at 80th Audio Engineering Society Convention (Montreux, 1986) preprint 2322(B-3)
4. ISHIDA, Y., ONISHI, K., SUGIYAMA, K., INOUE, T. and TANAKA, K. (1985) On the signal format for the improved professional use 2-channel digital audio recorder. Presented at 79th Audio Engineering Society Convention (New York, 1985) preprint 2270(A-4)
5. ONISHI, K., SUGIYAMA, K., ISHIDA, Y., KUSONOKI, Y. and YAMAGUCHI, T. (1986) An LSI for Reed–Solomon encoder/decoder. Presented at 80th Audio Engineering Society Convention (Montreux, 1986) preprint 2316(A-4)
6. NAKAJIMA, H. and ODAKA, K. (1983) A rotary-head high-density digital audio tape recorder. *IEEE Trans. Consum. Electron.*, **CE-29**, 430–437

7. ITOH, F., SHIBA, H., HAYAMA, M. and SATOH, T. (1986) Magnetic tape and cartridge of R-DAT. *IEEE Trans. Consum. Electron.*, **CE-32**, 442–452

8. ARAI, T., NOGUCHI, T., KOBAYASHI, M. and OKAMOTO, H. (1986) Digital signal processing technology for R-DAT. *IEEE Trans. Consum. Electron.*, **CE-32**, 416–424

9. H-P/Sony (1988) DAT data storage format description

10. ODAKA, K., TAN, E.T. and VERMEULEN, B. (1988) *Designing a Data Storage Format for Digital Audio Tape* (DAT). Hewlett-Packard Ltd, Bristol

11. PEEK, J.B.H. (1985) Communications aspects of the Compact Disc digital audio system. *IEEE Commun. Mag.*, **23**, 7–15

12. VRIES, L.B. *et al.* (1980) The digital Compact Disc – modulation and error correction. Presented at 67th Audio Engineering Society Convention (New York, 1980) preprint 1674

13. VRIES, L.B. and ODAKA, K. (1900) CIRC – the error correcting code for the Compact Disc digital audio system. in *Digital Audio, op. cit.* 178–186

14. CHEN, P.P. (1986) The Compact Disk ROM: how it works. *IEEE Spectrum*, 44–49, April

15. SAKO, Y. and SUZUKI, T. (1986) Data structure of the compact disk-read-only memory system. *Applied Optics*, **25**, No 22, 3996–4000

16. SMPTE 226M *Proposed American National Standard for component digital television recording 19 mm type D-1 cassette format – dimensions of tape cassettes*

17. EBU Tech. 3252-E, *Standard for recording digital television signals on magnetic tape in cassettes*

18. BRUSH, R. (1988) Design considerations for the D-2 PAL composite DVTR. Presented at 7th IERE Video, Audio and Data Recording Conference, York. IERE Publ. No. 79, 141–148

Index

Advantages of digital recording, 1–5
Air gap, 15–16, 20, 25
Amble frames, 175
Ampex, 152, 204
Analog systems, 1–3
Audio, 5–6, 146–152
    concealment, 82–83
    in D-1 and D-2, 208–209
Autocorrelation function, 47
Azimuth angle, 24
Azimuth recording, 22–24, 59, 166

Bad-block files, 214
B-adjacent code, 119–121
Bandwidth, 10–11
Binary digits (bits), 3
Binary signals, 2
Binary FM, 49
Bit error rate (BER), 85
Bits (binary digits), 3
Block-completed convolutional code, 134
Burst correction, 110–111

CD (Compact Disc), 25–26, 36–38, 130,
    134, 142, 179–185
    frame contents, 185–191
    player structure, 191–195
CDROM, 196–200
C-format, 204
Channel code, 6, 45
Chinese-remainder theorem, 118
Clock content, 72
Clusters, 214

Code rate, 51
Codebook, 51
Codewords, 85, 87
Colour TV broadcasting, 200–201
Compact Disc, see CD
Composite digital, 141
Computers, 5
    disk drives, 82
    memories/storage, 99–100, 173–174
Concealment, 82–3, 212–213
Constraint length, 50
Contamination of tape, 8, 151, 154, 158,
    203
Convolutional code, block-completed, 134
Convolutional interleaving, 132, 134
Convolutional RLL codes, 61–64
Copying quality, 4
Correction by erasure, 110
Crossinterleaving, 135–137
Crosstalk, 22–24
Crossword code, 91
Curie temperature, 34
Cyclic codes, 101–110
Cyclic redundancy check (CRC) code, 103
Cyclic redundancy check character,
    (CRCC), 109
Cyclic redundancy codes, 108

D-1 DVTR, 130, 203–204, 207
    audio in, 208–209
    error correction in, 209–212
D-2 DVTR, 130, 204–208
    audio in, 208–209
    error correction in, 209–212

DASH, 61, 130, 135
Data separator, 45
Data storage, 5, 173–178, 196
Defect handling in disks, 213, 219
Defect skipping, 215–217
Degradations, 1–3
Density ratio (DR), 46
Detents, 46
Diffraction, 28–29, 30
Digital data storage (DDS), 173–178
Digital recording, 4–6
Digital sum value (DSV), 57
Direct-read-after-write (DRAW) disks, 27, 34–36
Disadvantages of digital recording, 8
Disk drives, 5, 25, 82
    computer, 82
    flying heads, 15–16
    laser, 39
Disks
    defect handling, 213, 219
    error correction, 218–219
    optical, 25–27
DRAW (direct-read-after-write) disks, 27, 34–36
Drop frame timecode, 201

Editing interleaved recordings, 137–139
EFM (8/14) code, 55, 122, 180
Equalization, 24–25
Equalizer, 20
Erasable optical disks, 27
Erasure, 36, 127, 212
    by overwriting, 23, 166
Error bursts, 81
Error correction, 85–86
    in D-1 and D-2, 209–212
    in disks, 218–219
Error handling, 81–82
Error mechanisms, 80–81
Error sensitivity, 79–80
Eye pattern, 43

Fairchild 9401, 108
Figure of merit (FoM), 47
Fire code, 112–119
Fixed heads, 13–15
Flux changes, 3–4, 13, 17–18
Flying heads in disk drives, 15–16
FM, 49–50
Frames, 148, 174–175
Frequency range, 8
Frequency shift keying (FSK), 49

Galois field, 106, 113, 121–122
Gated peak detector, 18
Gaussian distribution of noise, 84
Graceful degradation, 70–72
Gray code, 99
Group codes, 51–61
Guard bands, 22
Guard-band-less recording, 22

Hamming code, 91–94, 99–100
Hamming distance, 95–99
HDM-1 code, 61
HDM-2 code, 63
Head noise, 10–12
Head-to-tape speed, 10–12

Interference, 26–27
Interleaved recordings, editing, 137–139
Interleaving, 100, 130–135
Interpolation, 82–83
Intersymbol interference, 20

Jitter margin, 47
Jitter windows, 43–47

Laser disk drives, 39
Laser disks, 25–27
Lasers, 31–32
Lenses, 30
Light
    diffraction, 28–9, 30
    interference, 27
    polarization, 32–34, 35
    refraction, 28
Light-emitting diode (LED), 31
Locator, 127
Low disparity code, 60

Magnetic recording, 9–16
Magneto-optics, 34
Magneto-resistive head, 14–15
Manchester code, 49
Merging, 53
MFM, 50
Miller^2 code, 50
Minimum transition parameter (M), 51
Miscorrection, 93
Mitsubishi, 147
Modulo-2 arithmetic, 104–107

N-group writing, 178
Noise, 83–86
NTSC, 201, 202, 206, 207
Nyquist rate, 44

Open reel digital audio recording, 146–152
Optical cutoff frequency, 38
Optical disks, 25–27
Optical readout, 36–38
Optical theory, 27–31
Overwriting, 23, 166

PAL, 201, 202, 206, 207
Parity, 86–89
Partial response, 65–70
Partial-wrap, 161–162
PCM adaptors, 141–146
PCM-1610, 109, 142, 143
Peak shift distortion, 20, 25
Phase margin, 47
Phase-locked loops (PLL), 72
Playback, 17–21
Polarization, 32–34, 35
Polynomials, 104–106, 108
Postamble, 73–74
Preamble, 73–74
Precoding, 66
Precompensation, 20, 25
Prerecorded RDAT, 166–167
ProDigi, 58, 63, 135, 152–157
Product code, 91
Pseudo-random sequence, 64–65
Pseudo-video, 141, 143
Pulse code modulation, 3
Pulse crowding, 20
Pulse sharpener, 20
Puncturing the code, 117

Randomized NRZ, 64–65
RDAT, 23, 59, 61, 130, 161–165
    cassette, 158–160
    prerecorded, 166–167
    recording, 167–173
    as storage medium, 173–178
Read-after-write, 178
Read-modify-write cycle, 100, 137
Redundant bits, 87, 111
Reed-Solomon codes, 121–130
Refraction, 28
Retries, 82

Revectoring, 217–218
Reverse reading, 74, 76
Rotary-head recorders, 10
Rotary heads, 22–24
Run length, 53
Run-length-limited (RLL) codes, 53, 61–64

Sampling, 3
SECDED (single error-correcting double error-detecting) codes, 100
Sector skipping, 215
Sensitivity to error, 79–80
Separation loss, 25
Shuffle, 212–213
Slicing, 183
Slipper, 16
Sony, 142, 158
Splicing tape, 151
Stationary-head recorders, 10
Subcarrier, 201–202
Sync block, 167–168
Sync pattern, 76
Sync slippage, 74
Synchronizing, 72–76
Syndrome, 93
Systematic codeword, 93

Tape, 159, 204, 207
    backcoat, 8, 11–12
    consumption, 10, 59, 158
    contamination/damage, 8, 151, 154, 158, 203
    splicing, 151
Ternary signal, 66, 70
Thermomagneto-optics, 34–36
Thickness loss, 19
Timebase correction, 4
Timing errors, 20
Track width, 9, 11, 23
Tracking signals, 61
Transitions, 43
Trellis coding, 70
TV broadcasting, 200–201
Twisted-ring counter, 101

U-matic, 144–146

Video, 6, 200–208
    concealment, 83
Viterbi decoding, 69

Window margin, 47
WORM, 26, 219
Write-once-read-many (WORM) disks,
   26, 219
Wyner-Ash code, 89–91

X-80, 147

2/3 code, 54
2/4 M code, 63, 153
4/5 code, 53
4/6 M code, 58
8/10 code, 59–60, 122, 176
8/14 (EFM) code, 55, 122, 180